the g.i. diet COOKBOOK

RICK GALLOP

RANDOM HOUSE CANADA

To my wife, Ruth, for her enthusiasm and encouragement, as well as the many hours spent in the kitchen, which helped make this book possible.

 Published in 2006 by Random House Canada, a division of Random House of Canada Limited. Distributed in Canada by Random House of Canada Limited.

www.randomhouse.ca

LIBRARY AND ARCHIVES CANADA CATALOGUING IN PUBLICATION

Gallop, Rick
The G.I. diet cookbook : 200 easy, delicious recipes for permanent weight loss / Rick Gallop.

Includes index.
ISBN-13: 978-0-679-31440-0
ISBN-10: 0-679-31440-7

1. Reducing diets—Recipes. 2. Glycemic index. I. Title.

RM222.2.G3425 2006 613.2'5 641.5'635 C2006-903004-9

Printed and bound in Canada

10 9 8 7 6 5 4 3 2 1

Contents

Introduction

Welcome to the fabulous world of G.I. eating, a world where you slim down to your ideal weight while eating three square meals plus three snacks a day; where you eat until you are full; where no food groups are eliminated and dessert is allowed; and where you will be the healthiest you've ever been. This may sound too good to be true, but it *is* true, and it's the reason *The G.I. Diet* has become an international bestseller, with over 1.5 million copies in print in a dozen languages. Thousands of G.I. Dieters have written to me about their weight-loss success, and they often tell me that the program shouldn't even be called a diet, simply a different way of eating. I think this is because people have had such bad experiences with previous diets that they've come to associate dieting with unappetizing, bland and difficult-to-prepare meals. Not so with the G.I. Diet!

With the *G.I. Diet Cookbook,* you will discover what a wide range of delicious foods and flavour combinations you can enjoy as you lose those unwanted pounds. I have been fortunate to have found a talented chef, Laura Buckley, to develop the recipes in this book. She trained at the Stratford Chefs School in Ontario and has worked in the kitchens of some of the top restaurants in Toronto. She has worked with me and my wife, Ruth, to build upon our family's favourite meals as well as the thousands of recipe suggestions we've received from readers. By using fresh herbs, exciting spices, ethnic flavours and wonderful produce, Laura has created over 200 appetizers, soups, salads, pastas, entrées, side dishes, breakfasts, muffins, breads and desserts. All of these recipes are sure to become family favourites—and there's no reason you shouldn't serve these dishes to your family, because the G.I. Diet is a nutritious and delicious way for everyone to eat, no matter their age or whether they need to lose weight.

Most of the recipes in this book can be made in less than 30 minutes, and some can be prepared in even less time. Some breakfast recipes, like Breakfast in a Glass, can be made virtually on the run, while others, like Berry-Stuffed French Toast or Baked Eggs in Ham Cups, are for relaxed weekend mornings. There are lots of soup, salad and sandwich choices for lunches, and a whole range of meatless, seafood, poultry and meat dishes for dinner. Because desserts are encouraged on the G.I. Diet, we have given you a generous range of delectable choices, including Chocolate Pudding, Rhubarb-Ginger Cobbler and Almond Cheesecake. Snacks—an essential part of the G.I. program—can be found in the Appetizers and Snacks section and the Muffins and Breads section. A few of our favourites are Warm Artichoke Dip, Spinach Bites and Chocolate Zucchini Muffins.

With all of these tempting recipes to try, you may wonder whether you really can lose weight while eating this fabulous food. The answer is a definite yes! In Part One: The G.I. Diet in a Nutshell, I give a short summary of how the diet works, explaining why you don't have to go hungry to lose weight. If you're new to the program, you'll probably want to read my book *The G.I. Diet* for a more comprehensive explanation. But if you've already read it, you may want to fast-forward to Part Two: The Recipes.

If you wish to write me about your experiences, please go to my website, www.gidiet.com, where you will also find the latest news on the G.I. Diet, readers' comments, professional feedback, and health and nutrition news. You can also subscribe there to my free quarterly newsletter.

My family had a field day trying out all these recipes. I hope you enjoy them as much as we do. I'd love to hear your comments.

PART I

The G.I. Diet in a Nutshell

CHAPTER ONE

Why Have We Become So Fat?

Nearly 56 percent of Canadians are overweight, and our obesity rate has doubled over the past twenty years. What's happening to us? Why, in a relatively short time, have we gained so much weight? Diet books in the past have specified various reasons. In the eighties, we were told that we had too much fat in our diet. Most recently we were told that fat wasn't the problem; it was actually carbohydrates. But both these explanations proved to be far too simplistic, and we soon realized that eating a low-fat or high-protein diet wasn't the solution for our collective weight crisis.

At its most basic, our problem is that we're consuming more calories than we're expending, and the resulting surplus is stored around our waists, hips and thighs as fat. But to explain why we're consuming more calories, we need to get back to basics and look at the three fundamental elements of our diet: carbohydrates, fats and proteins. We'll start with carbohydrates, since the popularity of low-carb diets like the Atkins program has made them a hot topic and given them a bad rap. Though they've been blamed for all our weight problems, their role in weight control has been greatly misunderstood.

Carbohydrates

Carbohydrates are a necessary part of a healthy diet. They are rich in fibre, vitamins and minerals, including antioxidants, which we now know play an important role in the prevention of heart disease and cancer. Carbohydrates are also the primary source of energy for our bodies. They are found in grains, vegetables, fruits, legumes (beans) and dairy products. Here is how carbs work: when you eat an orange or a bagel, your body digests the carbohydrates in the food and turns them into glucose, which provides you with energy. The glucose dissolves in your bloodstream and then travels to the parts of your body that use energy, such as your muscles and brain. So carbs are critical to everyone's health. What is important to realize when managing weight, however, is that not all carbs are the same.

Some carbohydrates break down into glucose in our digestive system at a slow and steady rate, gradually releasing their nutrients and keeping us feeling full and satisfied. Others break down rapidly, spiking our glucose levels and then disappearing quickly, leaving us feeling hungry again. For example, old-fashioned, large-flake oatmeal and cornflakes are both carbohydrates, but we all know the difference between eating a bowl of oatmeal for breakfast and eating a bowl of cornflakes. The oatmeal stays with you—it "sticks to your ribs" as my mother used to say—whereas your stomach starts rumbling an hour after eating the cornflakes, propelling you toward your next snack or meal. If, throughout the course of a day, you are eating carbs that break down rapidly, like cornflakes, as opposed to those that break down slowly, you will be eating more and, as a result, will begin to put on weight. If, however, you start eating carbs that break down slowly, like old-fashioned oatmeal, you will eat less and begin to lose weight. Selecting the right type of carb is key to achieving your optimum energy and weight. But how do you know which carbohydrate is the right type and which isn't?

Well, the first clue is the amount of processing that the food has undergone. The more a food is processed beyond its natural, fibrous state, the less processing your body has to do to digest it. And the quicker you digest the food the sooner you feel hungry again. This helps explain why the number of Canadian adults who are overweight has grown exponentially over the past fifty years. A hundred years ago, most of the food people ate came straight from the farm to the dinner table. Lack of refrigeration and scant knowledge of food chemistry meant that most food remained in its original state. However, advances in science, along with the migration of many women out of the kitchen and into the workforce, led to a revolution in prepared foods. Everything became geared to speed and simplicity of preparation. The giant food companies—Kraft, Kellogg's, Del Monte, Nestlé—eagerly met this need. We happily began spending more money for the convenience of prepared, processed, packaged, canned, frozen and bottled food. The Kraft Dinner era had begun.

It was during this period that the miller's traditional wind and water mills were replaced with high-speed steel rolling mills, which stripped away most of the key nutrients, including the bran, fibre and wheat germ (which could spoil), to produce a talcum-like powder: today's white flour. This fine white flour is the basic ingredient for most of our breads and cereals, as well as for baked goods and snacks such as cookies, muffins, crackers and pretzels. Walk through any supermarket and you are surrounded by towering stacks of these flour-based processed products. We're eating more and more of these foods; over the past three decades, our consumption of grain has increased by 50 percent. Our bodies are paying the price for this radical change in eating habits.

The second clue in determining whether a carbohydrate is the right type is the amount of fibre it contains. Fibre, in simple terms, provides low-calorie filler. It does double duty, in fact: it literally fills up your stomach, so you feel satiated, and it acts as a protective barrier against digestive juices, helping to slow down the digestive process. There are two forms of fibre: soluble and insoluble. Soluble fibre is found in carbs like oatmeal, beans, barley and citrus fruits, and has been shown to lower blood cholesterol levels. Insoluble fibre is important for normal bowel function and is typically found in whole wheat breads, cereals and most vegetables.

Two other important components, fats and proteins, inhibit the rapid breakdown of food in our digestive system. Let's look at fats first.

Fats

Fat, like fibre, acts as a brake in the digestive process. When combined with other foods, fat becomes a barrier to digestive juices. It also signals the brain that you are satisfied and do not require more food. Does this mean that we should eat all the fat we want? Definitely not!

Though fat is essential for a nutritious diet, and contains various key elements that are crucial to the digestive process, cell development and overall health, it also has twice the number of calories per gram as carbohydrates and protein. For example, if you decide to "just add peanut butter" to your otherwise disciplined regime, it doesn't take much—two tablespoons—to spike your total calorie count by a couple hundred calories, or about 10 percent of your total daily calorie intake. As well, once you eat fat, your body is a genius at hanging onto it and refusing to let it go. This is because the body stores reserve supplies of energy in fat, usually around the waist, hips and thighs. Fat is money in the bank as far as the body is concerned—a rainy-day investment for when you have to call up extra energy. This clever system originally helped our ancestors survive during periods of famine. The problem today is that in developed countries we don't live with cycles of feast and famine—it's more like feast, and then feast again! But the body's eagerness for fat continues, along with its reluctance to give it up.

This is why losing weight is so difficult: your body does everything it can to persuade you to eat more fat. How? Through fat's capacity to make things taste good. Juicy steaks, chocolate cake and rich ice cream do taste better than a bean sprout because of their fat content.

Sorry to say, there's no getting around it: if you want to lose weight, you have to watch your fat consumption. In addition, you need to be concerned about the type of fat you eat; many fats are harmful to your health. There are four types of fat: the best, the good, the bad and the really ugly. The "really ugly" fats are potentially the most dangerous, and they lurk in many of our most popular snack foods, baked goods, crackers and cereals. (You can spot them by checking labels for "hydrogenated" or "partially hydrogenated" oils.)

The "bad" fats are called saturated fats, and almost always come from animal sources. Butter, cheese and meat are all high in saturated fats. There are a couple of others that you should be aware of: coconut oil and palm oil are two vegetable oils that are saturated, and because they are cheap, they are used in many snack foods, especially cookies. Saturated fats, such as butter or cheese, are solid at room temperature. They elevate your risk of heart disease and Alzheimer's, and the evidence is also growing that many cancers, including colon, prostate and breast, are associated with diets high in saturated fats.

The "good" fats are the polyunsaturates, and they are cholesterol free. Most vegetable oils, such as corn and sunflower, fall into this category. What you really should be eating, however, are the monounsaturated fats, which actually promote good health. These are the fats found in olives, almonds, and canola and olive oils. Monounsaturated fats have a beneficial effect on cholesterol and are good for your heart. This is one reason the incidence of heart disease is low in Mediterranean countries, where olive oil is a staple. Although fancy olive oil is expensive, you can enjoy the same health benefits from less costly supermarket brands. Olive oil doesn't have to be extra virgin, double cold pressed.

Another highly beneficial oil that falls into its own category is omega-3, a fatty acid that is found in deep-sea fish—such as salmon, mackerel, albacore tuna and herring—as well as in lake trout, walnuts, and flaxseed and canola oils. Some brands of eggs and liquid eggs also contain omega-3, which can help lower cholesterol and protect your cardiovascular health.

So "good" fats are an important part of a healthy diet and also help slow down digestion. Still, they're fat and they pack a lot of calories. We have to be careful, then, to limit our intake of polyunsaturated fats like almonds and olives when trying to lose weight. Since protein also acts as a brake in the digestive process, let's look at it in more detail.

Protein

Protein is an absolutely essential part of your diet. In fact, you are already half protein: 50 percent of your dry body weight comprises muscles, organs, skin and hair, all forms of protein. We need protein to build and repair body tissues, and it figures in nearly all metabolic reactions. Protein is also a critical brain food, providing amino acids for the neurotransmitters that relay messages to the brain. That's why it's not a good idea to skip breakfast on the morning of a big meeting or exam. Protein is literally food for thought.

The main sources of dietary protein come from animals: meat, seafood, dairy and eggs. Vegetable sources include beans and soy-based products like tofu. Unfortunately, protein sources such as red meat and full-fat dairy products are also high in "bad," or saturated fats, which are harmful to your health. It is important that we get our protein from sources that are low in saturated fats, such as lean meats, skinless poultry, seafood, low-fat dairy products, liquid eggs, and tofu and other soy products. One exceptional source of protein is the humble bean. Beans are a perfect food, really; they're high in protein and fibre, and low in saturated fat. That's why many of the recipes in this cookbook contain beans. Nuts are another excellent source of protein that are relatively high in fat—so eat a handful rather than a bowlful.

Protein is very effective in satisfying hunger. It will help make you feel fuller longer, which is why you should always try to incorporate some protein in every meal and snack. This will help keep you on the ball and feeling satisfied.

Now that we know how carbohydrates, fats and proteins work in our digestive system and what makes us gain weight, let's use the science to put together an eating plan that will take off the extra pounds.

CHAPTER TWO

The G.I. Diet

The "G.I." in G.I. Diet stands for glycemic index, which is the basis of this diet (and the only scientific phrase you'll need to know). The glycemic index is the secret to reducing calories and losing weight without going hungry. It measures the speed at which carbohydrates break down in our digestive system and turn into glucose, the body's main source of energy or fuel.

The glycemic index was developed by Dr. David Jenkins, a professor of nutritional sciences at the University of Toronto, when he was researching the impact of different carbohydrates on the blood sugar, or glucose, level of diabetics. He found that certain carbohydrates broke down quickly and flooded the bloodstream with sugar, but others broke down more slowly, only marginally increasing blood sugar levels. The faster a food breaks down, the higher the rating on the glycemic index, which sets sugar at 100 and scores all other foods against that number. These findings were important to diabetics, who could then use the index to identify low-G.I., slow-release foods that would help control their blood sugar levels. Here are some examples of the G.I. ratings of a range of popular foods:

Examples of G.I. Ratings

High G.I.		Low G.I.	
Baguette	95	Orange	44
Cornflakes	84	All-Bran	43
Rice cake	82	Oatmeal	42
Doughnut	76	Spaghetti	41
Bagel	72	Apple	38
Cereal bar	72	Beans	31
Biscuit	69	Plain yogurt	25

What do these G.I. ratings have to do with the numbers on your bathroom scales? Well, it turns out that low-G.I., slow-release foods have a significant impact on our ability to lose weight. As I have explained, when we eat the wrong type of carb, a high-G.I. food, the body quickly digests it and releases a flood of sugar (glucose) into the bloodstream. This gives us a short-term high, but the sugar is just as quickly absorbed by the body, leaving us with a post-sugar slump. We feel lethargic and start looking for our next sugar fix. A fast-food lunch of a double cheeseburger, fries and a Coke delivers a short-term burst of energy, but by mid-afternoon we start feeling tired, sluggish and hungry. That's when we reach for a "one-time-only" brownie or bag of potato chips. These high-G.I. foods deliver the rush we want and then let us down again. The roller-coaster ride is a hard cycle to break. A high-G.I. diet will make you feel hungry more often, so you end up eating more and gaining more weight.

Let's look at the other end of the G.I. index. Low-G.I. foods, such as fruits, vegetables, whole grains, pasta, beans and low-fat dairy products, take longer to digest, deliver a steady supply of sugar to our bloodstream and leave us feeling fuller for a longer time. Consequently, we eat less. It also helps that most of these foods are lower in calories. As a result, we consume less food and fewer calories, without going hungry or feeling unsatisfied.

The key player in this process of energy storage and retrieval is insulin, a hormone secreted by the pancreas. Insulin does two things very well. First, it regulates the amount of sugar (glucose) in our bloodstream, removing the excess and storing it as glycogen for immediate use by our muscles, or putting it into storage as fat. Second, insulin acts as a security guard at the fat gates, reluctantly giving up its reserves. This evolutionary feature is a throwback to the days when our ancestors were hunter-gatherers, habitually experiencing times of feast or famine. When food was in abundance, the body stored its surplus as fat to tide it over the inevitable days of famine.

When we eat a high-G.I. food, our pancreas releases insulin to reduce the glucose level in our blood, which, if left unchecked, would lead to hyperglycemia. If we aren't using all the energy at that moment, the glucose is stored as fat. Soon we become hungry again. Our body can either draw on our reserves of fat and laboriously convert them back to sugar or it can look for more food. Since giving up extra fat is the body's last choice—who knows when that supply might come in handy!—our body would rather send us to the fridge than work to convert fat back to sugar. This helped survival back in the old days, but it gets in the way of weight loss now.

So our goal is to limit the amount of insulin in our system by avoiding high-G.I. foods, which stimulate its production, and instead choosing low-G.I. foods, which keep the supply of sugar in our bloodstream consistent. Slow-release, low-G.I. carbohydrates help curb your appetite by leaving you feeling fuller for a longer period of time. When you combine them with lean protein and the best fats, which help slow the digestive process, you have the magic combination that will allow you to lose weight without going hungry.

Translated into real food, what does this mean? Well, for dinner you could have a grilled chicken breast, boiled new potatoes, a side salad of romaine lettuce and red pepper, dressed with a bit of olive oil and lemon, and some asparagus. The trick is to stick with foods that have a low G.I., are low in fat and are lower in calories. This sounds—and is, in fact—quite complex. It might seem to you as though I'm breaking my promise of an easy weight-loss plan. But don't worry: I've done all the calculations, measurements and math for you, and sorted the foods you like to eat into one of three categories based on the colours of the traffic light. This easy-to-follow colour-coded system means you will never have to count calories or points, or weigh and measure food. The G.I. Diet's emphasis on fruits and vegetables, whole grains, low-fat dairy products, lean protein and the "best" fats is a nutritionally ideal way to eat and doesn't eliminate any food groups. It will keep you feeling satisfied and energetic as you slim down to your ideal weight.

Now let's get to the details: what to eat, how much and how often.

What Do I Eat?

To find out what to eat and what to avoid to start losing weight, check out The Complete G.I. Diet Food Guide on pages 16–24. Here's how the colour-coded categories work:

Red-Light Foods

The foods in the red column are to be avoided. They are high-G.I., higher-calorie foods.

Yellow-Light Foods

The foods in the yellow column are mid-range G.I. foods and should be regarded with caution. There are two phases in the G.I. Diet: Phase I is the weight-loss portion of the diet, and yellow-light foods should be avoided during this time.

Once you've reached your target weight, you enter Phase II, maintenance, and you can begin to enjoy yellow-light foods from time to time.

Green-Light Foods

The green column lists foods that are low-G.I., low in fat and lower in calories. These are the foods that will make you lose weight. Don't expect them to be tasteless and boring; there are many delicious and satisfying choices that will make you feel as though you aren't even on a diet.

If you're a veteran of the low-carbohydrate craze, you'll be surprised to find potatoes and rice in the green-light column; they are fine as long as they are the right type. Baked potatoes and French fries have a high G.I., while boiled, small new potatoes have a low G.I. Short-grain, glutinous rice served in Chinese and Thai restaurants is high-G.I., while long-grain, brown, basmati and wild rice are low. Pasta is also a green-light food—as long as it is cooked only until al dente (with some firmness to the bite). Any processing of food, including cooking, will increase its G.I., since heat breaks down a food's starch capsules and fibre, giving your digestive juices a head start. This is why you should never overcook vegetables; instead steam them or boil them in a small amount of water just until they are tender. This way they will retain their vitamins and other nutrients, and their G.I. rating will remain low.

Almost all the recipes in this book are green-light; however, I've indicated the few that are yellow-light. You will notice that some green-light recipes call for a yellow- or red-light ingredient. The quantity called for is so minor that it will have little to no effect on your blood sugar level. So don't worry—the recipes are still green-light.

How Much Do I Eat?

While following the G.I. program, you should be eating three meals and three snacks daily. Don't leave your digestive system with nothing to do. If your digestive system is busy processing food and steadily supplying energy to your brain, you won't be looking for high-calorie snacks. All of the recipes in the Appetizers and Snacks and Muffins and Breads sections in this book make perfect green-light snacks. Enjoy!

You can, but for a few exceptions that I outline at the top of the next page, eat as much of the green-light foods as you like—within reason (five heads of cabbage is a bit extreme).

Green-Light Servings

Crispbreads (with high fibre, e.g., Wasa Fibre)	2 crispbreads
Green-light breads (which have at least 2½ to 3 grams of fibre per slice)	1 slice
Green-light cereals	½ cup
Green-light nuts	8 to 10
Margarine (nonhydrogenated, light)	2 teaspoons
Meat, fish, poultry	4 ounces (about the size of a pack of cards)
Nuts	small handful
Olive/canola oil	1 teaspoon
Olives	4 to 5
Pasta	¾ cup cooked
Potatoes (new, boiled)	2 to 3
Rice (basmati, brown, long-grain)	⅔ cup cooked
PHASE II	
Chocolate (at least 70 percent cocoa)	2 squares
Red wine	1 5-ounce glass

Portions

Each meal and snack should contain, if possible, a combination of green-light protein, carbohydrates—especially fruit and vegetables—and fats. An easy way to visualize portion size is to divide your plate into three sections (see illustration below). Half the plate should be filled with vegetables; one quarter should contain protein, such as lean meat, poultry, seafood, eggs, tofu or legumes; and the last quarter should contain a green-light serving of rice, pasta or potatoes.

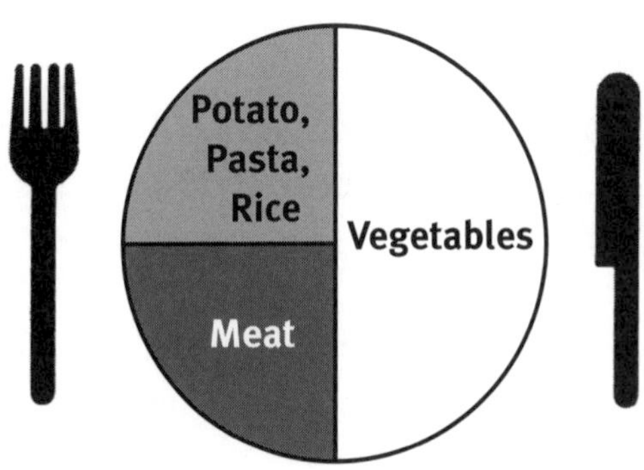

When Do I Eat?

Try to eat regularly throughout the day. If you skimp on breakfast and lunch, you will probably be starving by dinner and end up piling on the food. Have one snack mid-morning, another mid-afternoon and the last before bed. The idea is to keep your digestive system happily busy so you won't start craving those red-light snacks.

Note: Before starting any major change in your eating patterns, check with your doctor.

Phase II

Once you've reached your weight loss target, you enter Phase II of the G.I. Diet, which is the maintenance phase. At this point, you can ease up a bit on limiting portion and serving sizes and start adding some yellow-light foods to your diet. The idea is to get comfortable with your G.I. program: this is how you're going to eat for the rest of your life.

Of course, Phase II is also the danger zone, the stage when most diets go off the rails. Most people think that when they reach their weight-loss goal, they can just drop the diet and go back to their old eating habits. And frankly, when I take a close look at what many of these diets expect you to live on, I can understand why people can't stick to them for long. However, your new lighter body requires fewer calories, and your metabolism has become more efficient—your body has learned to do more with fewer calories than in its old spendthrift days. Keeping these two developments in mind, add a few more calories in Phase II, but don't go overboard. Don't make any significant changes in your serving sizes, and remember to make yellow-light foods the exception rather than the rule. (That is why almost all of the recipes in this book are green-light, with a few yellow-light exceptions.) This way, you will keep the balance between the calories you're consuming and the calories you're expending—and that is the secret to maintaining your new weight.

Making the G.I. program your diet for life shouldn't be a hardship, because it was designed to give you a huge range of healthy choices, so you won't feel hungry, bored or unsatisfied. You won't even be tempted to revert to your old ways, because if you should fall prey to a double cheeseburger, you will be dismayed at how heavy, sluggish and ungratified you feel afterward. You will be too attached to your new feeling of lightness and level of energy to abandon them.

The Complete G.I. Diet Food Guide

BEANS			
	Baked beans with pork		Baked beans* (low fat)
	Broad		Black beans
	Refried		Black-eyed peas
			Butter beans
			Chickpeas
			Italian
			Kidney
			Lentils
			Lima
			Mung
			Navy
			Pigeon
			Refried (low fat)
			Romano
			Soybeans
			Split peas

*** Limit serving size to 1/2 cup.**

BEVERAGES	Alcoholic drinks* Cocout milk Fruit drinks Milk (whole or 2%) Regular coffee Regular soft drinks Rice milk Sweetened juice Watermelon juice	Diet soft drinks (caffeinated) Milk (1%) Most unsweetened juice Red wine* Vegetable juices	Bottled water Club soda Decaffeinated coffee (with skim milk, no sugar) Diet soft drinks (no caffeine) Herbal tea Light instant chocolate Milk (skim) Soy milk (plain, low fat) Tea (with skim milk, no sugar)
BREADS	Bagels Baguette/ Croissants Cake/Cookies Cornbread Crispbreads (regular) Croutons English muffins Hamburger buns Hot dog buns Kaiser rolls Melba toast Muffins/Doughnuts Pancakes/Waffles Pizza Stuffing Tortillas White bread	Crispbreads (with fibre)* Pita (whole wheat) Tortillas (whole wheat) Whole-grain breads	100% stone-ground whole wheat* Crispbreads (with high fibre, e.g., Wasa Fibre)* Whole-grain, high-fibre breads (2½ to 3 g fibre per slice)*

*** Limit serving size (see page 13).**

CEREALS			
	All cold cereals except those listed as yellow- or green-light	Kashi Go Lean Crunch	100% Bran
	Cereal/Granola bars	Kashi Good Friends	All-Bran
	Granola	Shredded Wheat Bran	Bran Buds
	Grits		Cold cereals with minimum 10 g fibre per serving
	Muesli (commercial)		Fibre 1
			Fibre First
			Kashi Go Lean
			Oat Bran
			Porridge (large flake oats)
			Red River
CEREAL/GRAINS			
	Amaranth	Cornstarch	Arrowroot flour
	Almond flour	Spelt	Barley
	Couscous	Whole wheat couscous	Buckwheat
	Millet		Bulgur
	Polenta		Gram flour
	Rice (short-grain, white, instant)		Kamut (not puffed)
	Rice cakes		Quinoa
	Rice noodles		Rice (basmati, wild, brown, long-grain)
			Wheat berries
CONDIMENTS/SEASONINGS			
	Croutons	Mayonnaise (light)	Capers
	Ketchup		Chili powder
	Mayonnaise		Extracts (vanilla, etc.)
	Tartar sauce		Garlic
			Gravy mix (maximum 20 calories per 1/4 cup serving)
			Herbs
			Horseradish
			Hummus
			Mayonnaise (fat-free)

			Mustard Salsa (no added sugar) Sauerkraut Soy sauce (low sodium) Spices Teriyaki sauce Vinegar Worcestershire sauce
DAIRY			
	Almond milk Cheese Chocolate milk Coconut milk Cottage cheese (whole or 2%) Cream Cream cheese Evaporated milk Goat milk Ice cream Milk (whole or 2%) Rice milk Sour cream Yogurt (whole or 2%)	Cheese (low fat) Cream cheese (light) Frozen yogurt (low fat, low sugar) Ice cream (low fat) Milk (1%) Sour cream (light) Yogurt (low fat, with sugar)	Buttermilk Cheese (fat-free) Cottage cheese (1% or fat-free) Cream cheese (fat-free) Extra low-fat cheese (e.g., Laughing Cow Light, Boursin Light) Fruit yogurt (non-fat with sweetener) Ice cream (1/2 cup, low-fat and no added sugar, e.g., Breyers Premium Fat Free, Nestlé Legend Milk (skim) Sour cream (fat-free) Soy milk (plain, low fat) Soy cheese (low fat)
FATS AND OILS			
	Butter Coconut oil Hard margarine Lard Mayonnaise	Corn oil Mayonnaise (light) Most nuts Natural nut butters Natural peanut butter	Almonds* Canola oil*/seed Cashews* Flax seed Hazelnuts*

*** Limit serving size (see page 13).**

	Palm oil Peanut butter (regular and light) Salad dressings (regular) Tropical oils Vegetable shortening	Peanuts Pecans Salad dressings (light) Sesame oil Soft margarine (non-hydrogenated) Soy oil Sunflower oil Vegetable oils Walnuts	Macadamia nuts* Mayonnaise (fat-free) Olive oil* Pistachios* Salad dressings (low fat, low sugar) Soft margarine (non-hydrogenated, light)* Vegetable oil sprays
FRUITS			
FRESH	Cantaloupe Honeydew melon Kumquats Watermelon	Apricots Bananas Custard apples Figs Kiwi Mango Papaya Persimmon Pineapple Pomegranates	Apples Avocado* (1/4) Blackberries Blueberries Cherries Cranberries Grapefruit Grapes Guavas Lemons Nectarines Oranges (all varieties) Peaches Plums Pears Raspberries Rhubarb Strawberries
BOTTLED, CANNED, DRIED, FROZEN	All canned fruit in syrup Applesauce containing sugar Most dried fruit**	Canned apricots in juice or water Dried apples Dried apricots** Dried cranberries**	Applesauce (without sugar) Frozen berries Fruit spreads with fruit, not sugar as the main ingredient

*** Limit serving size (see page 13).**

**** For baking, it is OK to use a modest amount of dried apricots or cranberries.**

	(including dates and raisins)	Fruit cocktail in juice Peaches/Pears in syrup	Mandarin oranges Peaches/Pears in juice or water
JUICES*			
	Fruit drinks Prune Sweetened juice Watermelon	Apple (unsweetened) Cranberry (unsweetened) Grapefruit (unsweetened) Orange (unsweetened) Pear (unsweetened) Pineapple (unsweetened) Vegetable	
MEAT, POULTRY, FISH, EGGS AND TOFU			
	Beef (brisket, short ribs) Bologna Breaded fish and seafood Duck Fish canned in oil Goose Ground beef (more than 10% fat) Hamburgers Hot dogs Lamb (rack) Organ meats Pastrami (beef) Pâté Pork (back ribs, blade, spare ribs) Regular bacon Salami Sausages	Beef (sirloin steak, sirloin tip) Chicken/Turkey leg (skinless) Corn beef Dried beef Flank steak Ground beef (lean) Lamb (fore/leg shank, centre cut loin chop) Pork (centre loin, fresh ham, shank, sirloin, top loin) Turkey bacon Whole omega-3 eggs Tofu	All fish and seafood, fresh, frozen or canned (in water) Back bacon Beef (top/eye round steak) Chicken breast (skinless) Egg whites Ground beef (extra lean) Lean deli ham Liquid eggs (e.g., Break Free) Moose Pastrami (turkey) Pork tenderloin Sashimi Soy/Whey protein powder Soy cheese (low fat)

*** Whenever possible, eat the fruit rather than drink its juice.**

	Sushi Whole regular eggs		Tofu (low fat) Turkey breast (skinless) Turkey roll TVP (Textured Vegetable Protein) Veal Veggie burger Venison
PASTA			
	All canned pastas Gnocchi Macaroni and cheese Noodles (canned or instant) Pasta filled with cheese or meat Rice noodles		Capellini Fettuccine Macaroni Mung bean noodles Penne Rigatoni Spaghetti/Linguine Vermicelli
PASTA SAUCES			
	Alfredo Sauces with added meat or cheese Sauces with added sugar or sucrose	Sauces with vegetables (no added sugar)	Light sauces with vegetables (no added sugar, e.g., Healthy Choice)
SNACKS			
	Bagels Candy Cookies Crackers Doughnuts Flavoured gelatin (all varieties) French fries	Bananas Dark chocolate* (70% cocoa) Ice cream (low fat) Most nuts* Popcorn (air-popped microwaveable)	Almonds* Applesauce (unsweetened) Canned peaches/pears in juice or water Cottage cheese (1% or fat-free)

*** Limit serving size (see page 13).**

	Ice cream Muffins (commercial) Popcorn (regular) Potato chips Pretzels Pudding Raisins Rice cakes Sorbet Tortilla chips Trail mix White bread		Extra low-fat cheese (e.g., Laughing Cow Light, Boursin Light) Fruit yogurt (non-fat with sweetener) Food bars* Hazelnuts** Ice cream (1/2 cup, low fat and no added sugar, e.g., Breyers Premium Fat Free) Most fresh fruit Most fresh vegetables Most seeds Pickles Sugar-free hard candies
SOUPS			
	All cream-based soups Canned black bean Canned green pea Canned puréed vegetable Canned split pea	Canned chicken noodle Canned lentil Canned tomato	Chunky bean and vegetable soups (e.g., Campbell's Healthy Request, Healthy Choice, and Too Good To Be True) Homemade soups with green-light ingredients
SPREADS & PRESERVES			
	All products that have sugar as the first ingredient listed	Fructose Sugar alcohols	Fruit spreads (with fruit, not sugar, as the first ingredient) Marmite

*** 180–225 calorie bars, e.g., Zone or Balance Bars; 1/2 bar per serving**

*** * Limit serving size (see page 13).**

SUGAR & SWEETENERS

Corn syrup	Fructose	Aspartame
Glucose	Sugar alcohols	Equal
Honey		Splenda
Molasses		Stevia (note: not FDA approved)
Sugar (all types)		Sugar Twin
		Sweet'N Low

VEGETABLES

Broad beans	Artichokes	Alfalfa sprouts	Cauliflower
French fries	Beets	Asparagus	Celery
Hash browns	Corn	Beans (green/wax)	Collard greens
Parsnips	Potatoes (boiled)	Bell peppers	Cucumbers
Potatoes (instant)	Pumpkin	Bok choy	Eggplant
Potatoes (mashed or baked)	Squash	Broccoli	Fennel
Rutabaga	Sweet potatoes	Brussels sprouts	Hearts of palm
Turnip	Yams	Cabbage (all varieties)	Kale
		Carrots	Kohlrabi
		Mustard greens	Leeks
		Okra	Lettuce
		Olives*	Mushrooms
		Onions	Radicchio
		Peas	Radishes
		Peppers (hot)	Rapini
		Pickles	Snow peas
		Potatoes (boiled, new small)*	Spinach
			Swiss chard
			Tomatoes
			Zucchini

*** Limit serving size (see page 13).**

PART II

Recipes

Appetizers and Snacks

WASABI CHICKPEAS

These zesty chickpeas satisfy a craving for a savoury chip-like snack. Put them out in bowls for a party or have some on hand for an afternoon snack at the office.

2 tbsp	olive oil
2 tbsp	rice vinegar
2 tbsp	wasabi powder
1 tbsp	dry mustard
1/2 tsp	sesame oil
1/2 tsp	each salt and freshly ground pepper
2	cans (19 oz each) chickpeas, drained and rinsed

1. Preheat oven to 400°F.

2. In large bowl, whisk together oil, vinegar, wasabi powder, mustard, sesame oil, salt and pepper. Stir in chickpeas, tossing to coat well.

3. Spread mixture in single layer on parchment paper–lined baking sheet. Bake for 40 to 45 minutes or until golden.

Makes about 3 cups.

Make Ahead: Store in airtight container up to 3 days.

BABA GHANOUJ

Here's a lighter, but every bit as delicious, version of a party-dip favourite. Serve with raw veggies or whole wheat pita wedges.

1	large eggplant (about 1½ lb)
3	cloves garlic, minced
¼ cup	lemon juice
¼ cup	tahini
½ tsp	salt
¼ tsp	ground cumin
1 tbsp	extra-virgin olive oil
1 tbsp	chopped fresh parsley
¼ cup	black olives, such as Kalamata

1. Preheat oiled grill to medium-high and oven to 450°F.
2. Prick eggplant with fork in several places and grill, turning frequently, until skin blackens and blisters and flesh just begins to feel soft, 10 to 15 minutes. Transfer eggplant to baking sheet and bake for 15 to 20 minutes or until very soft. Set aside until cool enough to handle. Peel off skin and discard.
3. In food processor, blend eggplant, garlic, lemon juice, tahini, salt and cumin; process until smooth. (If mixture is too thick, thin with a little water or more lemon juice to desired consistency.)
4. Transfer mixture to serving bowl and use back of spoon to form shallow well. Drizzle oil over top and sprinkle with parsley. Arrange olives around side of bowl. Serve at room temperature.

Makes about 2 cups.

CREAMY VEGGIE DIP

You can serve this dip with pita or raw veggies, or use it as a tasty spread for whole-grain bread and crispbread.

8 oz	firm tofu
1/2 cup	grated carrot
1/2	red pepper, seeded and chopped
1	stalk celery, chopped
1/4 cup	roughly chopped parsley
2 tbsp	mustard
2 tbsp	low-fat mayonnaise
2 tsp	soy sauce

1. In blender or food processor, blend together all ingredients until smooth.

Makes about 2 cups.

Make Ahead: Refrigerate in airtight container up to 5 days.

RED LENTIL HUMMUS

This recipe works well either as a dip for veggies or Basmati Rice Crackers (see recipe, page 32) or as a sandwich spread.

3 cups	water
1 cup	dried red lentils, rinsed
1/3 cup	sun-dried tomatoes, rehydrated in hot water and drained
1/4 cup	tahini
3	cloves garlic, minced
1/2 tsp	each salt and freshly ground pepper
1/4 tsp	ground cumin
3 tbsp	extra-virgin olive oil
1 tbsp	lemon juice

1. In saucepan, bring water to boil. Add lentils and cook, uncovered, for 15 to 20 minutes or until tender; drain.
2. In food processor, pulse together cooked lentils, sun-dried tomatoes, tahini, garlic, salt, pepper and cumin until smooth. With food processor running, add oil and lemon juice.

Makes 2 cups.

Make Ahead: Refrigerate in airtight container up to 2 days.

Smokey Version: Add 1/4 tsp smoked paprika along with cumin.

BASMATI RICE CRACKERS

These crackers are best the day they are made, and are perfect for serving with dips.

1 tbsp	olive oil
1/4 cup	finely chopped onion
2	cloves garlic, minced
2 cups	chicken stock (low fat, low sodium)
1 cup	brown basmati rice
1/4 tsp	salt

1. In saucepan, heat oil over medium heat. Add onion and garlic and cook for 2 minutes or until softened. Add stock, rice and salt; bring to boil. Reduce heat to low, cover and cook for 45 minutes or until liquid is absorbed. Remove from heat and let sit for 10 minutes. Remove to bowl and allow to cool to room temperature.
2. Preheat oven to 375°F. Oil baking sheet.
3. Pour rice mixture out onto sheet of waxed paper. Cover with another sheet of waxed paper. Using rolling pin, roll out into rectangle about 12 x 9 inches and about 1/4 inch thick. Remove top sheet of waxed paper and cut rice mixture into triangular or rectangular pieces using sharp knife, or use 2-inch round cutter to cut out rounds. Carefully transfer to prepared baking sheet. Bake for 20 to 25 minutes or until crisp. Allow to cool completely on rack.

Makes 18 to 20 crackers.

WARM ARTICHOKE DIP

Always popular at parties, this dip can also be used cold as a spread for an open-faced sandwich.

1	pkg (10 oz) frozen chopped spinach, thawed and squeezed dry
1	can (14 oz) artichoke hearts, drained and chopped
1/2 cup	low-fat cottage cheese
1/4 cup	low-fat mayonnaise
1/4 cup	light cream cheese
3	cloves garlic, minced
1 tbsp	lemon juice
1 tbsp	grated Parmesan cheese
1/4 tsp	freshly ground pepper

1. Preheat oven to 375°F.

2. In bowl, stir together spinach, artichoke hearts, cottage cheese, mayonnaise, cream cheese, garlic, lemon juice, Parmesan and pepper. Transfer to 4-cup baking dish and bake for 20 to 25 minutes or until hot and bubbling.

Makes 3 cups.

Make Ahead: Refrigerate in airtight container up to 5 days. It reheats well in the microwave.

WHEAT AND OAT CRACKERS

Whip up a bunch of these crackers to serve with dips.

1 cup	large-flake oats
1 cup	whole wheat flour
1/2 tsp	salt
1/2 cup	warm water
1 tbsp	olive oil
2 tbsp	sesame seeds

1. Process oats, flour and salt in food processor until mixture is a fine-meal consistency. With motor running, pour in warm water and oil. Process until dough forms. Transfer to lightly floured surface and knead for 1 minute. Wrap dough in plastic wrap and allow to rest at room temperature for 30 minutes.
2. Preheat oven to 450°F.
3. Divide dough in half, keeping one half wrapped in plastic wrap. On lightly floured surface, roll out dough as thin as you can, keeping an even thickness. Carefully transfer to baking sheet. Repeat with remaining dough. Using clean spray bottle, or with your fingers, sprinkle surface of dough with a little water and then sesame seeds. Using pizza cutter or sharp knife, cut dough into rectangles about 2 x 3 inches.
4. Bake for 10 minutes or until crackers start turning golden brown. Crackers will crisp as they cool.

Makes about 24 crackers.

Make Ahead: Store in airtight container up to 1 month.

Variations:
After dough forms in food processor, mix in 1 tbsp dried herbs or cracked black pepper to taste.
Substitute caraway seeds for sesame seeds.

SAVOURY BISCOTTI

Dunk these savoury treats in soup or have them as a mid-afternoon snack with some raw veggies and cottage cheese. If your sun-dried tomatoes are very dry, soften them in hot water for 5 minutes, drain and squeeze dry.

1 1/2 cups	whole wheat flour
1/2 cup	wheat bran
1/3 cup	finely chopped sun-dried tomatoes
2 tbsp	grated Parmesan cheese
1 tsp	baking powder
1 tsp	dried oregano
1 tsp	freshly ground pepper
1/2 tsp	baking soda
1/2 cup	liquid egg
1/4 cup	olive oil
2 tbsp	water

1. Preheat oven to 350°F. Line baking sheet with parchment paper.
2. In large bowl, stir together flour, wheat bran, sun-dried tomatoes, Parmesan, baking powder, oregano, pepper and baking soda. In another bowl, whisk together egg, oil and water. Stir into flour mixture to form dough. If necessary, add up to 1 tbsp more water to make dough moist but not sticky.
3. Divide dough into 2 equal portions and place on prepared baking sheet. With lightly floured hands, press each portion into firm log about 2 to 2 1/2 inches wide, flattening tops slightly.
4. Bake for 20 minutes or just until firm. Let cool for 10 minutes.
5. Reduce oven temperature to 325°F. Using serrated knife, cut logs on diagonal into 1/2-inch thick slices. Place on baking sheet, leaving 1 inch between pieces. Bake until completely dry and crunchy, about 25 minutes, turning once.

Makes about 20 biscotti.

Make Ahead: Store in airtight container up to 5 days or freeze up to 1 month.

SPICY TORTILLA CHIPS

A nice spicy snack.

1 tbsp	olive oil
2 tsp	curry paste
4	small whole wheat tortillas

1. Preheat oven to 400°F.
2. In small bowl, whisk together oil and curry paste. Brush tortillas with mixture. Cut each tortilla into 8 triangles and place on baking sheet. Bake for 5 minutes or until crisp.

Makes 4 to 6 servings.

OVEN-FRIED ZUCCHINI COINS

A healthful alternative to the favourite deep-fried appetizer, snack or side dish.

3/4 cup	cornmeal
1/2 cup	whole wheat flour
2 tbsp	grated Parmesan cheese
1/2 tsp	each salt and freshly ground pepper
4	medium zucchini, cut into 1/2-inch rounds
2	egg whites, lightly beaten
1 tsp	olive oil

1. Preheat oven to 475°F.
2. In large plastic bag, combine cornmeal, flour, Parmesan, salt and pepper.
3. Dip zucchini in egg whites then shake in bag to coat.
4. Brush baking sheet with oil and arrange zucchini in single layer on baking sheet. Bake for 8 minutes. Flip and continue cooking for another 8 minutes or until golden brown and crisp.

Makes 4 to 6 servings.

SPINACH BITES

These make a great snack, hors d'oeuvre or even lunch when paired with a salad.

1 tbsp	olive oil
1	small onion, finely chopped (about 1/2 cup)
2	cloves garlic, minced
1	jalapeño pepper, seeded and finely chopped
6 cups	fresh spinach, chopped
1 cup	low-fat cottage cheese
1	omega-3 egg
1 tbsp	grated Parmesan cheese
1/2 tsp	salt
1/4 tsp	freshly ground pepper
1/2 cup	sunflower seeds, chopped
3/4 cup	dry whole wheat breadcrumbs

1. Preheat oven to 425°F.
2. In large non-stick frying pan, heat 2 tsp oil over medium-high heat. Cook onion, garlic and jalapeño until softened, about 5 minutes. Add spinach and cook, stirring, for another 5 minutes or until wilted and soft. Remove from heat and set aside to cool.
3. In large bowl, mix together cottage cheese, egg, Parmesan, salt and pepper. Stir in spinach mixture until well combined. Stir in sunflower seeds.
4. Place breadcrumbs on large plate. Scoop 1 tbsp of spinach mixture and place on top of breadcrumbs. Cover with crumbs and gently form into a ball with your hands (mixture will be slightly mushy). Place on baking sheet lightly coated with remaining oil. Repeat with remaining mixture. Bake for 20 minutes or until golden and crisp.

Makes 20.

Make Ahead: Freeze on baking sheet, then transfer to airtight container and freeze up to 2 months. Reheat at 375°F for 15 minutes or until hot.

SMOKED TROUT PÂTÉ

Spread this pâté on whole wheat crackers, pita or bread.

12 oz	smoked trout, broken into chunks
2 oz	light cream cheese, softened
1	shallot, finely chopped
2 tbsp	prepared horseradish
2 tbsp	lemon juice
1/2 tsp	freshly ground pepper

1. In food processor, purée trout, cream cheese, shallot, horseradish, lemon juice and pepper until smooth.

Makes 1 1/2 cups.

Make Ahead: Refrigerate up to 3 days.

CRAB NORI CONES

These are a fun party appetizer. The filling is also good wrapped in lettuce leaves or in a whole wheat pita.

2 tbsp	light mayonnaise
1 tbsp	prepared horseradish
1 tbsp	Dijon mustard
1 tbsp	lime juice
1 tsp	grated lime zest
Pinch	each salt and freshly ground pepper
2 cups	crabmeat
1	avocado, chopped
1/2	red pepper, seeded and diced
1/4 cup	chopped green onions
1/4 cup	chopped cilantro
2 tbsp	chopped fresh mint
6	sheets toasted nori

1. In bowl, whisk together mayonnaise, horseradish, mustard, lime juice and zest, salt and pepper. Fold in crabmeat, avocado, red pepper, green onions, cilantro and mint until well combined.
2. Using scissors, cut nori sheets into quarters. On each quarter, place large tablespoonful of filling close to one corner. Fold that corner over, then roll into cone. Seal overlapping sides with a few drops of water.

Makes 24.

Soups

GAZPACHO

This flavourful summer dish is a cross between a soup and a salad.

1 lb	tomatoes, seeded and chopped
2	stalks celery, chopped
1	red pepper, seeded and chopped
1	red onion, chopped
1	English cucumber, chopped
2	cloves garlic, minced
1 1/2 cups	vegetable cocktail
1/4 cup	red wine vinegar
1/4 cup	chopped cilantro
1/4 tsp	freshly ground pepper

1. In large bowl, stir together tomatoes, celery, red pepper, red onion and cucumber.
2. Transfer half of the mixture to blender or food processor and add garlic, 1/2 cup vegetable cocktail, and vinegar. Purée until almost smooth. Pour back into bowl with other half of vegetables and stir in remaining vegetable cocktail, cilantro and pepper. Refrigerate for at least 1 hour before serving.

Makes 8 servings.

Make Ahead: Refrigerate up to 1 day.

CHILLED SPINACH AND WATERCRESS SOUP

This creamy soup makes a delightful start to a summer meal.

3 cups	vegetable stock (low fat, low sodium)
4 cups	chopped fresh spinach
1 cup	chopped watercress
1 cup	buttermilk
1 cup	water chestnuts, chopped
1/4 cup	non-fat sour cream
2 tbsp	chopped fresh mint
1	clove garlic, minced
1/2 tsp	each salt and freshly ground pepper

1. Bring stock to simmer in large soup pot. Add spinach and watercress and cook for 3 minutes or just until wilted. Remove from heat and allow to cool slightly.
2. Stir in buttermilk, water chestnuts, sour cream, mint, garlic, salt and pepper.
3. In blender or food processor, purée 2 cups of soup until smooth. Stir back into remaining soup. Refrigerate for at least 2 hours or until chilled.

Makes 4 to 6 servings.

Make Ahead: Refrigerate up to 1 day.

MISO AND SEA VEGETABLE SOUP

Sea vegetables, such as kombu and arame, are a good source of calcium and other nutrients. If they are not available in your area, just follow the variation below.

6 cups	water
3	pieces kombu (6 inches each)
2 tsp	canola oil
1 cup	thinly sliced carrots
1/2 cup	finely chopped leek (white and light-green parts only), (see helpful hint on page 48)
1/2	red pepper, seeded and chopped
6 oz	shiitake mushrooms, stemmed and thinly sliced
2 tsp	minced fresh ginger
1/2 cup	arame, (soaked in 1 cup water for 10 minutes, then drained)
1/3 cup	miso
2	green onions, chopped

1. In large soup pot, combine water and kombu. Bring to boil; reduce heat and simmer for 20 minutes. Remove kombu and discard.
2. Meanwhile, in non-stick frying pan, heat oil over medium heat. Cook carrots, leek, red pepper, mushrooms and ginger for 5 minutes or until softened. Stir in arame. Add vegetables to broth.
3. In small bowl, whisk together miso and 1 cup of broth taken from soup pot; stir back into soup. Add green onions and simmer for 1 minute (do not allow to boil; it will destroy the flavour and beneficial enzymes in miso).

Makes 6 servings.

Variation: If kombu and arame are not available, replace water and kombu broth with hot chicken or vegetable stock. Replace arame with 1 bag (10 oz) baby spinach. Add to broth when adding vegetables. Simmer for 5 minutes or until spinach is tender.

HOT AND SOUR SOUP

Here's an easy G.I. version of the Chinese takeout classic.

3/4 cup	dried shiitake mushrooms
1 cup	boiling water
6 cups	vegetable stock
1 tbsp	minced fresh ginger
1	clove garlic, minced
8 oz	firm tofu, cut into 1/4-inch cubes
1	carrot, thinly sliced
1/2 cup	shredded cabbage
1/2 cup	shelled edamame or peas
1/4 cup	rice vinegar
2 tbsp	cornstarch
2 tbsp	soy sauce
1/2 tsp	freshly ground pepper
1 tsp	sesame oil
2	egg whites, lightly beaten
1/2 cup	chopped green onions
1/4 cup	chopped cilantro

1. In small bowl, cover shiitakes with boiling water; let stand for 10 minutes. Drain and slice thinly.

2. In soup pot, bring stock, ginger and garlic to boil. Add tofu, carrot, cabbage and edamame; reduce heat and simmer for 10 minutes or until vegetables are tender.

3. In small bowl, whisk together vinegar, cornstarch, soy sauce and pepper until smooth. Add mixture to soup; bring to boil. Cook for 2 minutes, stirring constantly, or until mixture thickens slightly. Stir in sesame oil. Slowly pour in egg whites, stirring constantly. Garnish with green onions and cilantro.

Makes 6 servings.

MUSHROOM SOUP WITH ROASTED GARLIC AND GINGER

This soup tastes even better the next day, after the flavours have had time to blend. For a heartier dish, add chopped cooked chicken, cooked shrimp or cubed tofu.

1/4 cup	dried porcini mushrooms
1/4 cup	dried shiitake mushrooms
1 cup	boiling water
1	head garlic
1 tbsp	canola oil
8 oz	fresh shiitake mushrooms, stemmed and sliced
4 cups	chicken stock or vegetable-based "chicken" stock (low fat, low sodium) (see note on page 47)
2 tbsp	minced fresh ginger
2 tbsp	rice vinegar
1 tbsp	soy sauce
2 tsp	mirin or dry sherry
1/4 tsp	freshly ground pepper
1/4 cup	chopped green onions

1. Preheat oven to 375°F.
2. In bowl, soak dried mushrooms in boiling water for 30 minutes; drain and reserve liquid.
3. Meanwhile, cut slice off top of garlic to expose cloves. Wrap garlic in foil and bake for 30 minutes or until cloves are completely soft. Squeeze softened garlic into small bowl, discarding papery husk, and set aside.
4. In soup pot, heat oil over medium-high heat. Add fresh shiitake mushrooms and cook for 5 minutes or until softened. Add stock, dried mushrooms and soaking liquid, roasted garlic, ginger, vinegar, soy sauce, mirin and pepper; stir. Bring to boil, reduce heat and cook, covered, for 20 minutes. Stir in green onions.

Makes 4 servings.

TOMATO-FENNEL SOUP

The flavour of this soup improves with age, so leftovers will taste even better.

4 cups	chicken stock (low fat, low sodium) or vegetable-based "chicken" stock
5	cloves garlic, sliced
1 lb	fennel bulb, chopped
1	onion, chopped
1	can (28 oz) chopped tomatoes
1	can (19 oz) cannellini (white kidney) beans, drained and rinsed
1 tbsp	chopped fresh thyme
1/4 tsp	each salt and freshly ground pepper

1. In large soup pot, combine chicken stock, garlic, fennel, onion, tomatoes, cannellini beans, thyme, salt and pepper; bring to boil. Reduce heat to simmer and cook for 25 minutes or until fennel is tender.

Makes 6 servings.

Make Ahead: Refrigerate up to 3 days.

Note: There are several vegetarian "chicken"- or "beef"-flavoured stocks available that can be used in place of meat-based stock.

ORANGE-SCENTED BROCCOLI AND LEEK SOUP

The unusual combination of ingredients gives this soup personality.

2 tbsp	olive oil
4 cups	thinly sliced leeks (white and light-green parts only) (see helpful hint below)
6 cups	chicken stock or vegetable-based "chicken" stock (low fat, low sodium) (see note on page 47)
6 cups	broccoli florets, cut into small pieces
1 cup	large-flake oats
	Zest of 1 medium orange
1/2 tsp	red pepper flakes
1/2 tsp	each salt and freshly ground pepper
2 cups	skim milk
1/2 cup	shredded light-style cheddar cheese (optional)
	Freshly ground pepper

1. In large soup pot, heat oil over medium-high heat. Cook leeks for 7 to 8 minutes or until softened and golden brown. Add stock, broccoli, oats, orange zest, red pepper flakes, salt and pepper. Bring to boil; reduce heat and simmer, covered, for 30 minutes or until vegetables are soft. Stir in milk; continue to cook for another 10 minutes.
2. Serve each bowlful with sprinkle of cheddar cheese, if desired, and freshly ground pepper.

Makes 6 to 8 servings.

Helpful Hint: To clean leeks, cut dark green part off and remove any outer layers. Trim root end. Cut leek in half lengthwise and rinse under water to remove any dirt. Pat dry.

WINTER VEGETABLE SOUP WITH SPINACH

A nutritious soup to fend off winter's chill.

2 tsp	olive oil
3	medium carrots, chopped
2	cloves garlic, chopped
1	onion, chopped
1 lb	celeriac (also known as celery root), chopped
1	large sweet potato, chopped
1 tsp	dried thyme
1/2 tsp	dried rosemary
6 cups	chicken or vegetable stock (low fat, low sodium)
3/4 cup	small pasta shapes (such as ditali or tubetti)
1/2 tsp	each salt and freshly ground pepper
1	bag (10 oz) baby spinach

1. In large soup pot, heat oil over medium-high heat. Cook carrots, garlic, onion, celeriac, sweet potato, thyme and rosemary for 8 minutes or until vegetables are starting to soften and turn golden.
2. Pour in stock and bring to boil. Reduce heat, cover and simmer, stirring occasionally, for 25 minutes or until vegetables are tender.
3. Working in batches, purée soup in blender or food processor until smooth, then return to pot. Bring to boil and add pasta, salt and pepper. Reduce to a simmer and cook for about 5 minutes. Add spinach and cook for another 5 minutes or until pasta is tender.

Makes 6 servings.

SQUASH AND APPLE SOUP

The apple in this soup adds a touch of sweetness—and the ginger a nice zing.

1 tbsp	olive oil
2½ lb	butternut squash, peeled, seeded, cut into ½-inch cubes (about 6 cups)
1 cup	chopped leeks (white and light-green parts only) (see helpful hint on page 48)
1	onion, chopped
1	medium carrot, cut into ½-inch cubes
1 tbsp	minced fresh ginger
1 tbsp	chopped fresh thyme
½ tsp	dried sage
1	large apple, peeled, cored and cut into ½-inch cubes
4 cups	chicken or vegetable stock (low fat, low sodium)
1 cup	apple juice
1	can (19 oz)cannellini (white kidney) beans, drained and rinsed
	Chopped fresh chives

1. In large soup pot, heat oil over medium-high heat. Add squash, leeks, onion, carrot, ginger, thyme and sage; cook for 10 minutes or until vegetables are slightly softened. Stir in apple.
2. Pour in stock and apple juice and bring to boil. Reduce heat, cover and simmer, stirring occasionally, for 20 minutes or until vegetables are tender.
3. Pour half of soup into blender or food processor and purée until smooth. Return to pot over medium heat. Add beans and cook for 2 minutes or until heated through. Serve sprinkled with chopped chives.

Makes 8 servings.

ROASTED TOMATO AND BEAN SOUP WITH BACON

Roasting the vegetables really brings out their sweetness and flavour.

1 lb	plum tomatoes, halved lengthwise
1	onion, cut into chunks
1	carrot, cut into 2-inch chunks
4	cloves garlic
1 tbsp	olive oil
1 tsp	ground cumin
2½ cups	chicken or vegetable stock (low fat, low sodium)
1	can (19 oz) black beans, drained and rinsed
3	slices Canadian bacon, chopped
½ tsp	each salt and freshly ground pepper

1. Preheat oven to 375°F.
2. In roasting pan, toss together tomatoes, onion, carrot, garlic, oil and cumin. Roast until vegetables are starting to brown, stirring occasionally, about 1 hour. Remove carrot; chop and set aside. Place remaining vegetables in blender or food processor along with stock. Purée mixture until smooth with some small chunks remaining.
3. Transfer soup to saucepan. Stir in reserved carrot, beans, bacon, salt and pepper; bring to simmer. Cook for 5 minutes or until heated through.

Makes 6 servings.

SPINACH AND MEATBALL SOUP

This soup is a meal in a bowl. You can double the meatball recipe and freeze them on trays. Once frozen, store them in resealable freezer bags. Add frozen meatballs to the soup and cook for 5 to 10 minutes longer.

Meatballs:

1	omega-3 egg
1	small onion, grated
1/4 cup	fresh whole wheat breadcrumbs
2 tbsp	chopped fresh parsley
1	clove garlic, minced
1 tsp	ground cumin
1 tsp	salt
1/2 tsp	freshly ground pepper
1/2 lb	extra-lean ground beef

Soup:

2 tbsp	olive oil
1	onion, chopped
1	clove garlic, minced
1	bag (10 oz) baby spinach
1/4 cup	chopped fresh parsley
2 tbsp	chopped cilantro
2 tbsp	tomato paste
1/4 tsp	ground cumin
6 cups	chicken or beef stock (low fat, low sodium)
1/4 tsp	each salt and freshly ground pepper
1	can (19 oz) cannellini (white kidney) beans, drained and rinsed
3 tbsp	lemon juice
1/2 cup	Yogurt Cheese (optional) (see recipe, page 248)

1. **Meatballs:** In bowl, whisk egg with fork. Add onion, breadcrumbs, parsley, garlic, cumin, salt and pepper; stir to combine. Add meat and combine well, using hands to distribute ingredients evenly. Using a teaspoon, shape mixture into balls and set aside.

2. **Soup:** In large soup pot, heat oil over medium-high heat. Add onion and garlic and cook for 4 to 5 minutes or until softened. Stir in spinach, parsley, cilantro, tomato paste and cumin and continue cooking for another 2 minutes, or until spinach is wilted. Add stock, salt and pepper. Add meatballs and beans; bring to boil. Reduce heat, cover and simmer for 20 minutes or until meatballs are no longer pink inside. Stir in lemon juice. Serve with a dollop of Yogurt Cheese, if desired.

Makes 6 servings.

VEGETABLE BARLEY SOUP AU PISTOU

"Pistou" is just French for pesto, but it makes this soup sound oh so continental. You can used bottled pesto, but why not make your own with the recipe provided?

1 tbsp	olive oil
2	carrots, chopped
2	stalks celery, chopped
1 cup	chopped leeks (white and light-green parts only) (see helpful hint on page 48)
1 cup	chopped zucchini
1/2	red pepper, seeded and chopped
2	sprigs fresh thyme
6 cups	chicken stock or vegetable-based "chicken" stock (low fat, low sodium) (see note on page 47)
3/4 cup	cut fresh or frozen green beans
1/2 cup	barley
2 tbsp	tomato paste
1/2 tsp	salt
1/4 tsp	freshly ground pepper
1/3 cup	G.I. Pesto (see recipe, page 55)

1. In large soup pot, heat oil over medium heat; cook carrots, celery, leeks, zucchini, red pepper and thyme for about 8 minutes or until softened.
2. Add stock, green beans, barley, tomato paste, salt and pepper; bring to boil. Reduce heat, cover and simmer for 45 minutes or until barley is tender. Remove thyme stalks and stir in pesto.

Makes 6 servings.

Variation: Add 1 cup of chopped cooked turkey or chicken to the soup, or try different pestos, such as sun-dried tomato or arugula.

G.I. PESTO

The addition of water along with the oil in this pesto reduces the fat content. It gives the pesto a lighter green colour than traditional pesto, but it still tastes great.

2 cups	packed fresh basil leaves
3	cloves garlic
1/3 cup	sunflower seeds
1/4 cup	grated Parmesan cheese
1 1/2 tbsp	lemon juice
1/4 tsp	each salt and freshly ground pepper
3 tbsp	water
3 tbsp	extra-virgin olive oil

1. In blender or food processor, purée basil, garlic, sunflower seeds, Parmesan, lemon juice, salt and pepper. With motor running, add water and oil in steady stream.

Makes 3/4 cup.

Make Ahead: Refrigerate in airtight container up to 3 days or freeze up to 6 months.

Helpful Hint: When basil is plentiful, make extra batches and freeze in ice-cube trays. When frozen, remove from tray and store in airtight container in freezer. You'll always have a bit of pesto on hand to stir into hot pasta or soups.

HAM AND SPLIT PEA SOUP

This thick, homey soup warms your soul on a chilly day.

8 cups	water
2 cups	split peas, rinsed and sorted
4 oz	cooked lean ham, chopped
4	onions, chopped
3	carrots, chopped
3	stalks celery, chopped
1 tbsp	chopped fresh thyme
1	bay leaf
1/2 tsp	each salt and freshly ground pepper

1. In large soup pot, combine water, split peas, ham, onions, carrots, celery, thyme, bay leaf, salt and pepper; bring to boil. Skim off any scum. Cover and simmer for 1 1/2 to 2 hours or until peas are soft.

Makes 8 servings.

Make Ahead: Freeze up to 3 months.

LEMONY LENTIL AND RICE SOUP

The lemon juice in this easy-to-prepare soup provides a lively, fresh flavour.

1 tbsp	olive oil
1	onion, chopped
1	clove garlic, minced
1 cup	chopped carrot
2 tsp	curry powder (or to taste)
8 cups	chicken stock or vegetable-based "chicken" stock (low fat, low sodium) (see note on page 47)
1 cup	dried green lentils (preferably du Puy), rinsed
1/2 cup	brown basmati rice
1 tbsp	chopped fresh thyme
1	bay leaf
1/4 cup	fresh lemon juice
1/4 tsp	each salt and freshly ground pepper

1. In large heavy soup pot, heat oil over medium heat; cook onion and garlic until softened, about 3 minutes. Add carrot and curry powder; cook for 2 minutes.
2. Add stock, lentils, rice, thyme and bay leaf; simmer, covered, for 40 to 45 minutes or until lentils and rice are tender. Remove bay leaf. Add lemon juice, salt and pepper.

Makes 8 servings.

SCALLOP AND SNOW PEA SOUP

This is an easy, light and refreshing soup.

6 cups	chicken stock or vegetable-based "chicken" stock (low fat, low sodium) (see note on page 47)
3	cloves garlic, crushed
1	2-inch piece ginger, sliced
1 tbsp	soy sauce
2 tsp	fish sauce
2 tsp	mirin
1 tsp	hot chili sauce (or to taste)
8 oz	snow peas, strings removed and cut into 1-inch pieces
1	carrot, shredded
12 oz	bay scallops (or sea scallops, halved)
3	green onions, finely sliced

1. In large soup pot, bring stock, garlic and ginger to boil. Cover and simmer for 15 minutes. Remove ginger and garlic and discard.
2. Add soy sauce, fish sauce, mirin and chili sauce. Bring to boil. Add snow peas and carrot. Cook for 2 minutes. Add scallops; cook for 2 minutes or just until scallops are opaque. Stir in green onions.

Makes 6 servings.

Make Ahead: You can make the recipe up to the end of Step 1 a day ahead and refrigerate, then reheat before finishing soup.

Variation: Substitute small, peeled raw shrimp for the scallops.

QUICK AND EASY CHICKEN NOODLE SOUP

Why buy canned soup when you can make this simple homemade version?

2 tsp	olive oil
2	carrots, chopped
2	stalks celery, chopped
3	cloves garlic, chopped
1	onion, chopped
1 tbsp	chopped fresh thyme
6 cups	chicken stock (low fat, low sodium)
12 oz	boneless chicken breast, diced
1 cup	frozen peas
3/4 cup	small pasta shapes
1/4 cup	chopped fresh parsley
1/4 tsp	each salt and freshly ground pepper

1. In large soup pot, heat oil over medium-high heat. Add carrots, celery, garlic, onion and thyme and cook for 10 minutes or until vegetables are slightly softened.

2. Pour in stock and bring to boil. Reduce heat to simmer and add chicken, peas and pasta. Simmer for 15 minutes or until chicken is no longer pink inside and pasta is al dente. Stir in parsley. Season with salt and pepper.

Makes 6 servings.

CREAMY SEAFOOD CHOWDER

Don't be alarmed by the long ingredient list; this chowder is simple to make and definitely worth it.

2 tbsp	olive oil
1	onion, chopped
1	clove garlic, minced
2	stalks celery, chopped
1	large carrot, chopped
1/4 cup	whole wheat flour
3 cups	fish or chicken stock
8	mini new potatoes (about 1/2 lb), skins on, halved
2 tsp	chopped fresh oregano (or 1/2 tsp dried)
4	bay leaves
1/2 tsp	each salt and freshly ground pepper
1/2 lb	haddock fillet or other mild-flavoured firm-fleshed fish, cut into chunks
1/2 lb	raw shrimp or scallops (or mixture of both)
1 cup	skim milk
1 cup	fresh or frozen corn kernels
1/4 cup	chopped fresh parsley
2 tbsp	grated Parmesan cheese
1/2 cup	non-fat sour cream (optional)

1. In large heavy soup pot, heat oil over medium heat; cook onion and garlic until softened, about 3 minutes. Add celery and carrot; cook for 2 minutes. Stir in flour; cook, stirring, for 1 minute. Add stock, potatoes, oregano, bay leaves, salt and pepper and bring to boil; reduce heat and simmer, covered, for 15 minutes or until potato is tender.

2. Add haddock and shrimp; cook for 3 minutes or until opaque. Stir in milk and corn; heat through. Stir in parsley and Parmesan. Serve with a dollop of sour cream, if using.

Makes 6 to 8 servings.

ASIAN-STYLE BEEF NOODLE SOUP

Partially freeze the sirloin to make it easier to slice thinly, or look for fast-fry strips in the supermarket.

1	1-inch piece fresh ginger
1	whole star anise
1/2	cinnamon stick
3	whole cloves
1/4 tsp	peppercorns
4 cups	beef stock (low fat, low sodium)
1 cup	water
1	small head bok choy, chopped
4 oz	mung bean vermicelli
2 tsp	soy sauce
2 tsp	canola oil
12 oz	top sirloin, thinly sliced
1 cup	bean sprouts
1/4 cup	chopped fresh basil

1. Wrap ginger, anise, cinnamon, cloves and peppercorns in square of cheesecloth. Place in soup pot with stock and water and bring to boil; reduce heat and simmer for 30 minutes. Remove and discard cheesecloth pouch. Add bok choy, vermicelli and soy sauce. Cook until tender, about 4 minutes.
2. Meanwhile, in non-stick frying pan, heat oil over high heat. Stir-fry beef until just browned on outside, about 2 minutes. Add to soup pot along with any juices. Ladle soup into bowls and sprinkle with bean sprouts and basil.

Makes 6 servings.

CHICKEN AND SMOKED OYSTER GUMBO

This hearty stew-like soup makes a satisfying one-pot meal.

1/4 cup	canola oil
12 oz	boneless chicken breast, cut into bite-size pieces
2	cloves garlic, minced
2	stalks celery, chopped
1	onion, chopped
1	green pepper, seeded and chopped
2	stalks celery, chopped
1	pkg (8 oz) frozen okra, thawed
2 tbsp	whole wheat flour
2 cups	chicken stock (low fat, low sodium)
1	can (28 oz) diced tomatoes
2	bay leaves
1/4 tsp	each salt and freshly ground pepper
2	cans (3.75 oz each) smoked oysters, drained
3 cups	cooked long-grain brown or basmati rice

1. In large soup pot, heat 1 tbsp oil over medium-high heat. Add chicken and cook, stirring, until browned, about 5 minutes. Remove to bowl.
2. Add remaining oil to pot. Add garlic, celery, onion, green pepper and okra; cook until vegetables are softened, about 8 minutes. Stir in flour and cook, stirring constantly until deep golden brown, 3 to 4 minutes. Add stock, tomatoes, bay leaves, salt and pepper; bring to boil. Reduce heat and simmer for 10 minutes.
3. Add reserved chicken and oysters; cook until heated through, about 2 minutes. Remove bay leaves and ladle soup into bowls over rice.

Makes 6 servings.

Make Ahead: Freeze up to 2 months.

Salads

RAITA SALAD

This recipe is based on the refreshing Indian condiment. Try serving this salad with the Coffee- and Spice-Rubbed Chicken Breasts (see recipe, page 165).

1	bag (10 oz) baby spinach
1	medium English cucumber, quartered lengthwise and sliced into 1/2-inch chunks
2	tomatoes, chopped
1/2	red onion, thinly sliced
1 cup	low-fat yogurt
1/2 tsp	ground cumin
1/4 tsp	salt

1. In large bowl, toss together spinach, cucumber, tomatoes and red onion.
2. In another bowl, stir together yogurt, cumin and salt. Add to spinach mixture and toss to coat.

Makes 4 servings.

ROASTED FENNEL AND ORANGE SALAD

This is somewhere between a salad and a side dish. Serve it with grilled fish.

2	medium bulbs fennel
2	oranges
1/2 cup	pitted black olives
1 cup	dry white wine or vermouth
3 tbsp	olive oil
3	cloves garlic, minced
1 tbsp	grated orange zest
1 tsp	fresh thyme leaves
1/2 tsp	each salt and freshly ground pepper

1. Preheat oven to 375°F.
2. Trim feathery tops from fennel and reserve for garnish. Trim base of fennel. Cut each bulb into quarters lengthwise and then each quarter in half lengthwise. In pot of boiling salted water, cook fennel for 5 minutes; drain and place in baking dish or roasting pan large enough to hold fennel in single layer.
3. Cut slice from top and bottom of each orange and discard. Cut away peel from oranges so no white pith remains. Slice into 1/4-inch thick rounds. Add to fennel along with olives.
4. In small bowl, whisk together wine, oil, garlic, orange zest, thyme, salt and pepper. Pour evenly over fennel mixture. Cook in top third of oven for 30 to 40 minutes or until fennel is tender and golden at edges. Garnish with reserved fennel tops. Serve hot or at room temperature.

Makes 4 to 6 servings.

CAESAR SALAD

We all need a Caesar salad in our recipe repertoire. No one will guess that tahini is the secret ingredient that makes this green-light version every bit as creamy as Chef Caesar Cardini's original.

3	slices whole-grain bread
2 tsp	olive oil
Pinch	each salt and freshly ground pepper
1	large head romaine lettuce

Dressing:

3	cloves garlic, minced
3	anchovy fillets, finely minced
2 tbsp	tahini
1 tsp	Dijon mustard
1/2 tsp	Worcestershire sauce
1/2 tsp	each salt and freshly ground pepper
3 tbsp	lemon juice
2 tbsp	warm water
1 1/2 tbsp	extra-virgin olive oil

1. Preheat oven to 350°F.
2. Cut bread into 1/2-inch pieces and place in bowl. Add oil, salt and pepper and toss to coat well. Arrange in single layer on rimmed baking sheet. Bake for 20 minutes or until golden and crisp. Let cool.
3. Tear lettuce into bite-size pieces; place in large bowl.
4. **Dressing:** In small bowl, stir together garlic, anchovies, tahini, mustard, Worcestershire sauce, salt and pepper. Whisk in lemon juice, water and oil.
5. Pour dressing over lettuce and toss to coat. Sprinkle with croutons.

Makes 4 servings.

MIXED GREENS WITH ROASTED PEARS, PECANS AND CHÈVRE

Roasting the pears makes them extra sweet.

3	ripe but firm Bosc pears
2 tsp	olive oil
8 cups	mixed salad greens (including radicchio, arugula and frisée)
1/2 cup	toasted pecan halves
2 oz	chèvre (goat cheese), crumbled

Dressing:

2 tbsp	apple juice
1 tbsp	balsamic vinegar
1/2 tsp	honey or Splenda
Pinch	each salt and freshly ground pepper
3 tbsp	extra-virgin olive oil

1. Preheat oven to 425°F.
2. Quarter and core pears. Cut each quarter in half lengthwise. Toss pears with oil and place on baking sheet; bake for 15 to 20 minutes or until pears are tender and turning golden brown. Set aside to cool.
3. Wash and dry greens.
4. **Dressing:** In small bowl, whisk together apple juice, vinegar, honey, salt and pepper. Whisk in oil.
5. Toss salad greens with dressing. Divide among plates. Arrange pear slices over top of greens. Sprinkle with pecans and chèvre.

Makes 6 servings.

WARM SPINACH AND BACON SALAD WITH CRANBERRY VINAIGRETTE

This bistro-style salad makes a terrific lunch.

4 slices	back bacon
1	bag (10 oz) baby spinach
1	large apple, chopped
1/2 cup	cranberry juice
1 1/2 tbsp	red wine vinegar
1 tbsp	Dijon mustard
1/2 tsp	Splenda
1/4 tsp	each salt and freshly ground pepper
1/4 cup	dried cranberries
1/4 cup	roasted sunflower seeds

1. In non-stick frying pan, cook bacon over medium-high heat until browned. Let cool and chop into bite-size pieces.
2. In large bowl, toss together spinach and apple.
3. In small saucepan, whisk together cranberry juice, vinegar, mustard, Splenda, salt and pepper. Add cranberries and heat dressing until just warmed.
4. Pour dressing over salad and toss to coat. Sprinkle with bacon and sunflower seeds and toss again.

Makes 4 servings.

ESCAROLE AND BERRY SALAD WITH HERB AND LEMON VINAIGRETTE AND BLUE CHEESE

Choose escarole with tender, light green leaves; the dark leaves can be quite bitter.

1	head escarole, shredded (about 6 cups)
1/2 cup	fresh raspberries
1/2 cup	fresh blueberries
4	radishes, thinly sliced
2 oz	light-style blue cheese, crumbled

Dressing:

3 tbsp	extra-virgin olive oil
2 tbsp	lemon juice
1 tbsp	chopped fresh basil
1 tbsp	chopped fresh parsley
1 tbsp	chopped fresh mint
2 tsp	grated lemon zest
1 tsp	Splenda
1/4 tsp	each salt and freshly ground pepper

1. In large bowl, toss together escarole, raspberries, blueberries and radishes.
2. **Dressing:** In bowl, whisk together oil, lemon juice, basil, parsley, mint, lemon zest, Splenda, salt and pepper.
3. Pour dressing over salad and toss to coat. Sprinkle with blue cheese and toss again.

Makes 4 to 6 servings.

MEDITERRANEAN SUMMER SALAD

This recipe from our daughter-in-law Jennifer is most delicious at the height of the summer. You can easily make substitutions. If you don't have yellow or orange peppers, use green or red peppers. Red onion can easily replace the sweet onion.

3	medium tomatoes, cut into chunks
1	English cucumber, cut into 1-inch chunks
1	yellow pepper, seeded and cut into 1-inch chunks
1	orange pepper, seeded and cut into 1-inch chunks
1/2	sweet onion (such as Vidalia), thinly sliced
1/2 cup	pitted black olives
1/2 cup + 2 tbsp	shredded fresh basil
1/2 cup	chopped fresh parsley
1/4 cup	extra-virgin olive oil
3 tbsp	balsamic vinegar
1/4 tsp	each salt and freshly ground pepper
4 oz	light-style feta cheese, crumbled (about 1 cup)

1. In large bowl, mix together tomatoes, cucumber, peppers, onion, olives, 1/2 cup basil and parsley. Add oil, vinegar, salt and pepper; toss gently.
2. Just before serving, sprinkle with feta and remaining basil.

Makes 4 to 6 servings.

Make Ahead: If you prefer a more marinated salad, you can complete Step 1 several hours in advance.

BROCCOLI AND CAULIFLOWER SALAD

Here's a deliciously different way to serve these nutrient-packed veggies. You can substitute any fresh herb you want for the tarragon.

6 cups	broccoli florets
6 cups	cauliflower florets
1/4 cup	extra-virgin olive oil
3 tbsp	lemon juice
2 tbsp	Dijon mustard
2 tsp	chopped fresh tarragon
1/4 tsp	freshly ground pepper
Pinch	salt
1	red onion, chopped

1. In steamer basket placed over pot of boiling water, cook broccoli and cauliflower for about 5 minutes or until tender-crisp.
2. In large bowl, whisk together oil, lemon juice, mustard, tarragon, pepper and salt. Add broccoli, cauliflower and red onion; toss to coat. Allow to marinate for at least 30 minutes before serving.

Makes 4 servings.

Make Ahead: Refrigerate up to 3 days.

CELERIAC SLAW

This is a nice change from the usual cabbage coleslaw. Look for celeriac (also known as celery root) that is firm and heavy for its size, with few roots and knobs for easier peeling. Work as quickly as possible because peeled celeriac tends to discolour.

1	celeriac, peeled and grated
1	large apple, unpeeled, grated
1 cup	thinly sliced celery
1	green or red pepper, seeded and chopped
2	green onions, chopped
1/4 cup	chopped fresh parsley
1/4 cup	sunflower seeds

Dressing:

1/4 cup	extra-virgin olive oil
3 tbsp	low-fat mayonnaise
2 tbsp	white wine vinegar
1 tbsp	grainy mustard
1 tbsp	lemon juice
1/2 tsp	each salt and freshly ground pepper

1. In large bowl, combine celeriac, apple, celery, green pepper, green onions, parsley and sunflower seeds.
2. **Dressing:** In another bowl, whisk together oil, mayonnaise, vinegar, mustard, lemon juice, salt and pepper. Pour over salad and toss.

Makes 6 servings.

Make Ahead: Refrigerate up to 1 day.

COTTAGE CHEESE SALAD

This creamy, crunchy salad can also be stuffed into a whole wheat pita.

2 cups	low-fat cottage cheese
1/2 cup	grated carrot
1/2 cup	grated celery
1/2 cup	grated radish
2	green onions, chopped
1	large apple, cored and chopped
2 tsp	minced fresh ginger
2 tsp	soy sauce
1	clove garlic, minced
1 tsp	rice vinegar
1/2 tsp	toasted sesame oil

1. In bowl, stir together cottage cheese, carrot, celery, radish, green onions, apple, ginger, soy sauce, garlic, vinegar and sesame oil.

Makes 4 servings.

FENNEL WALDORF SALAD

This salad is an appealing mix of tastes and textures. Look for leafy, very fresh watercress.

3	stalks celery, sliced
2	apples, unpeeled, cored and sliced
1	large navel orange, peeled and segmented
1 cup	red or green seedless grapes
1	small bulb fennel, thinly sliced
4 cups	watercress
1/3 cup	shelled pistachios, chopped

Dressing:

1/4 cup	low-fat plain yogurt
2 tbsp	low-fat mayonnaise
2 tbsp	lemon juice
2 tsp	canola oil
1 tsp	grated lemon zest
Pinch	each salt and freshly ground pepper

1. In large bowl, toss together celery, apples, orange, grapes, and fennel.
2. **Dressing:** In small bowl, whisk together yogurt, mayonnaise, lemon juice, oil, lemon zest, salt and pepper.
3. Pour dressing over fruit and vegetables and toss to coat. Garnish with watercress and pistachios.

Makes 4 servings.

COLD NOODLE SALAD WITH CUCUMBER AND SESAME

These refreshing noodles pair well with Ginger-Wasabi Halibut (see recipe, page 131).

6 oz	thin pasta (vermicelli, capellini or spaghettini)
1 tbsp	rice vinegar
4 tsp	Splenda
2 tsp	soy sauce
1/2	English cucumber, quartered lengthwise, seeded and thinly sliced
2 tbsp	toasted sesame seeds

1. In large pot of boiling salted water, cook pasta until al dente, about 4 minutes. Drain and rinse under cold water. Place in large bowl.
2. In small bowl, stir together vinegar, Splenda and soy sauce. Pour over cooked noodles and stir in cucumber and sesame seeds; toss well to coat.

Makes 6 servings.

WILD RICE SALAD

Crunchy and citrusy, this salad can be made ahead of time.

1 cup	wild rice
1	orange, peeled, segmented and chopped
1/4 cup	chopped dried apricots
1/4 cup	chopped almonds
1/4 cup	chopped fresh parsley

Dressing:

1/4 cup	orange juice
2 tbsp	extra-virgin olive oil
1 tbsp	white wine vinegar
2 tsp	Dijon mustard
1/4 tsp	each salt and freshly ground pepper

1. In large pot of boiling salted water, cook wild rice, covered, until tender, 35 to 40 minutes. Drain and transfer to large bowl. Add orange, apricots, almonds and parsley.
2. **Dressing:** In another bowl, whisk together orange juice, oil, vinegar, mustard, salt and pepper. Pour over rice mixture and toss to combine. Let cool; cover and refrigerate at least 2 hours before serving.

Makes 4 servings.

Make Ahead: Refrigerate up to 2 days.

LEMONY GRILLED VEGETABLE PASTA SALAD

This is a lovely side dish for chicken or fish. Toss in some leftover roast chicken or a can of tuna or salmon for a simple lunch.

1/3 cup	chopped shallots
1/4 cup	olive oil
1/4 cup	lemon juice
2 tbsp	Dijon mustard
2 tbsp	chopped fresh herbs (choose from a mixture of thyme, rosemary, oregano and marjoram)
1 tbsp	grated lemon zest
1/4 tsp	each salt and freshly ground pepper
1	small eggplant, quartered, then cut crosswise into 1/2-inch thick slices
1	each red pepper and yellow pepper, seeded and cut into 1/2-inch pieces
1	zucchini, halved and cut into 1/2-inch rounds
1	red onion, cut into wedges
1	carrot, cut into 1/4-inch thick rounds
6 oz	shiitake mushrooms, stems discarded and caps cut into quarters
3 cups	whole wheat penne or other similar-size pasta shape
2 tbsp	chopped fresh basil or parsley

1. Preheat oven to 425°F.
2. In large bowl, whisk together shallots, oil, lemon juice, mustard, herbs, lemon zest, salt and pepper. Add eggplant, peppers, zucchini, onion, carrot and mushrooms and toss to coat with dressing. Place on rimmed baking sheet and roast in oven for 25 to 30 minutes or until vegetables are golden and tender.
3. Meanwhile, in large pot of boiling salted water, cook pasta for 8 minutes or until al dente. Drain and transfer to large bowl. Add cooked vegetables and basil, tossing well. Serve warm or at room temperature.

Makes 4 to 6 servings.

Make Ahead: Refrigerate up to 3 days.

BLACK BEAN TABBOULEH

This is another wonderful recipe from our daughter-in-law Jennifer. It's a light, satisfying salad that can also be served as a main course. As well, you can use it as the stuffing in a whole wheat tortilla or in lettuce wraps.

1 cup	bulgur
1 tsp	salt
2 cups	boiling water
1	can (19 oz) black beans, drained and rinsed
4	plum tomatoes, chopped
1 cup	tightly packed fresh parsley, roughly chopped
1/2 cup	tightly packed fresh basil, chopped
1/4 cup	chopped green onions
1/4 cup	extra-virgin olive oil
2 tbsp	lemon juice
1/4 tsp	freshly ground pepper
	Lettuce leaves and lemon wedges

1. In large bowl, combine bulgur and 1/2 tsp salt. Pour boiling water over bulgur and stir to combine. Set stand for 15 to 20 minutes or until liquid is absorbed and bulgur is tender.
2. Stir black beans, tomatoes, parsley, basil and green onions into bulgur.
3. Drizzle oil and lemon juice over mixture; sprinkle with remaining salt and pepper. Stir to combine.
4. Line plates or platter with lettuce leaves and spoon salad over top. Garnish with lemon wedges.

Makes 6 servings.

Make Ahead: Refrigerate up to 2 days.

Variations:
Add 1 cucumber, chopped into bite-size pieces.
Substitute 1/2 cup chopped fresh cilantro for parsley.
Substitute 1/4 cup chopped fresh mint for parsley.

GRILLED SHRIMP AND PEAR SALAD

This light dish from our friend Meryle combines unexpected ingredients yielding delicious results.

4	pears, quartered, cored and sliced
1	red pepper, seeded and chopped
1	red onion, chopped
1/4 cup	chopped cilantro
1 lb	large raw shrimp, peeled and deveined
1 tbsp	oil
1 tsp	chopped fresh oregano

Dressing:

2 tbsp	rice vinegar
2 tbsp	orange juice
1 tsp	orange zest
1 tsp	honey or maple syrup

1. Preheat oiled grill or broiler to high.
2. **Dressing:** In large bowl, whisk together vinegar, orange juice, orange zest and honey.
3. Add pears, red pepper, red onion and cilantro to dressing; toss to coat. Set aside.
4. In bowl, toss shrimp with oil and oregano. If you plan to grill the shrimp, thread onto bamboo skewers that have been soaked in water for 30 minutes. If you plan to broil them, spread on baking sheet. Grill or broil shrimp, turning once, until pink and firm, about 4 minutes.
5. Divide salad mixture among plates and top with shrimp.

Makes 4 to 6 servings.

SALMON, RED POTATO AND ASPARAGUS SALAD

This colourful salad is perfect for a spring or summer lunch party.

1/2 lb	skinless salmon fillet
1 tbsp	olive oil
1/2 tsp	each salt and freshly ground pepper
8 oz	asparagus, tough ends removed and cut diagonally into 1-inch pieces
8 cups	salad greens or baby spinach
8 oz	new red potatoes, cooked and quartered
1 pint	grape or cherry tomatoes, cut in half
1 cup	light-style feta cheese
6	green onions, chopped
1/3 cup	chopped fresh mint
1/4 cup	chopped fresh basil
3 tbsp	chopped fresh dill

Vinaigrette:

1/3 cup	extra-virgin olive oil
3 tbsp	lemon juice
1 tsp	grated lemon zest
1/2 tsp	salt
1/4 tsp	freshly ground pepper

1. Preheat oiled grill to medium-high.
2. Brush salmon with oil; sprinkle with salt and pepper. Grill salmon, turning once, until opaque and flakes easily with a fork, about 4 minutes per side. Remove to plate and let cool to room temperature. (You can also bake the salmon in a 425°F oven until opaque and flakes easily with a fork, 10 to 12 minutes.)
3. In steamer basket placed over pot of boiling water, cook asparagus, covered, until tender-crisp, about 5 minutes. Rinse asparagus under cold water until cool. Set aside.
4. **Vinaigrette:** In small bowl, whisk together oil, lemon juice, lemon zest, salt and pepper.
5. On large platter, toss salad greens with 2 tbsp of the vinaigrette.

6. Break salmon into bite-size chunks and place in large bowl. Add asparagus, potatoes, tomatoes, feta, green onions, mint, basil and dill; carefully toss with remaining dressing. Spoon over greens.

Makes 4 to 6 servings.

Baba Ghanouj, page 29
Here's a lighter but every bit as delicious version of a party-dip favourite. Serve with raw veggies or whole wheat pita wedges.

Spinach Bites, page 38
These make a great snack, hors d'oeuvre or even lunch when paired with a salad.

Orange-Scented Broccoli and Leek Soup, page 48
The unusual combination of ingredients gives this soup personality.

Mediterranean Summer Salad, page 70
This salad is most delicious at the height of the summer.

Thai Red Curry Shrimp Pasta, page 89
The combination of curry spices, lime and cilantro
are hallmarks of Thai cooking.

Falafel with Yogurt-Mint Sauce, page 101
This Middle Eastern street-food favourite is usually deep-fried. This green-light version is lightly pan-fried in a small amount of olive oil to keep it crisp.

Eggplant Rolls with Tomato Sauce, page 122
These rolls capture the flavours of the Mediterranean.

Tuna Salad, page 141

This can be served in romaine lettuce leaves as pictured, in endive spears, or atop a slice of stone-ground whole wheat bread.

Pastas

CREAMY GARLIC FETTUCCINE WITH TOFU AND RAPINI

Wow, a green-light cream sauce! Rapini (also called broccoli rabe) looks like broccoli with slender stalks and more leaves. It has a stong, slightly bitter taste. You can use broccoli or chopped asparagus instead of the rapini.

1 cup	low-fat cottage cheese
1/4 cup	light cream cheese
2 tbsp	grated Parmesan cheese
1	clove garlic, minced
1/4 tsp	ground nutmeg
1/4 tsp	each salt and freshly ground pepper
1 tbsp	olive oil
2 cups	cubed firm tofu
6 oz	whole wheat fettuccine or linguine
1	bunch rapini, chopped

1. In blender or food processor, purée cottage cheese, cream cheese, Parmesan, garlic, nutmeg, salt and pepper until smooth.
2. In non-stick frying pan, heat oil over medium-high heat. Brown tofu on all sides for about 2 minutes; remove to plate.
3. In large pot of boiling salted water, cook fettuccine for 5 minutes. Add rapini and cook for 3 to 4 minutes or until fettuccine is al dente and rapini is tender-crisp. Drain well and return to pot. Add tofu and cheese mixture, tossing to coat well with sauce.

Makes 4 servings.

PASTA PUTTANESCA

Named after Italian "ladies of the night," this dish is full of the zesty flavours of the Mediterranean.

1	pint cherry tomatoes, cut in half
2	cloves garlic, minced
2 tsp	olive oil
2 tsp	balsamic vinegar
1 tsp	chopped fresh thyme
1/2 tsp	red pepper flakes
1/4 tsp	each salt and freshly ground pepper
2 tbsp	chicken stock
1	can (19 oz) chickpeas, drained and rinsed
1/4 cup	pitted chopped olives
3	anchovies, blotted dry, chopped
1 tbsp	capers, rinsed
6 oz	whole wheat spaghetti
1/4 cup	chopped fresh basil or parsley
2 tbsp	grated Parmesan cheese

1. Preheat oven to 425°F.
2. In bowl, toss together tomatoes, garlic, oil, vinegar, thyme, red pepper flakes, salt and pepper. Spread evenly on rimmed baking sheet and roast for 10 minutes.
3. Heat stock in non-stick frying pan over medium-high heat. Add tomato mixture along with any accumulated juice. Stir in chickpeas, olives, anchovies and capers.
4. In large pot of boiling salted water, cook spaghetti for 8 minutes or until al dente. Drain and return to pot. Add sauce and toss to coat. Stir in basil and Parmesan.

Makes 4 servings.

LEMON LINGUINE WITH SMOKED SALMON

This pasta is good even at room temperature. Try it with different vegetables, such as snow peas, edamame or broccoli florets.

1/4 cup	lemon juice
2 tbsp	olive oil
1 tbsp	grated lemon zest
1/4 tsp	freshly ground pepper
6 oz	whole wheat linguine
3/4 cup	fresh or frozen peas
6 oz	smoked salmon, chopped
2	green onions, chopped
1/4 cup	chopped fresh parsley

1. In large bowl, whisk together lemon juice, oil, lemon zest and pepper.
2. In large pot of boiling salted water, cook linguine for 5 minutes. Add peas and continue to cook for another 3 minutes or until pasta is al dente. Drain and add to bowl with lemon mixture. Add salmon, green onions and parsley; toss to combine.

Makes 4 servings.

THAI RED CURRY SHRIMP PASTA

The combination of curry spices, lime and cilantro are hallmarks of Thai cooking.

1 lb	large raw shrimp, peeled and deveined
1 tsp	Thai red curry paste
1 tbsp	olive oil
4	cloves garlic, minced
2	large tomatoes, skinned, seeded and chopped
3/4 cup	white wine
	Zest and juice of 1 lime
1/4 tsp	each salt and freshly ground pepper
2 tbsp	chopped cilantro
6 oz	whole wheat spaghettini or linguine
	Lime wedges

1. In bowl, toss shrimp with curry paste until well coated. Cover and refrigerate for at least 2 and up to 8 hours.
2. In large non-stick frying pan, heat oil over medium heat. Add garlic and cook just until starting to turn golden, 1 to 2 minutes. Add tomatoes, wine, lime zest and juice, salt and pepper; bring to boil, reduce heat and simmer until sauce reduces and thickens, about 8 minutes. Add shrimp and cook, stirring, until pink and firm, 3 to 4 minutes. Stir in cilantro.
3. Meanwhile, in large pot of boiling salted water, cook pasta until al dente, about 8 minutes. Drain and add pasta to shrimp mixture. Toss to coat with sauce. Serve with lime wedges.

Makes 4 servings.

CHICKEN AND ARUGULA CANNELLONI WITH ORANGE BÉCHAMEL

Fresh pasta sheets are much easier to fill than the dried cannelloni tubes.

2 tsp	olive oil
1 lb	ground chicken or turkey
1	onion, chopped
2	cloves garlic, minced
1	can (19 oz) romano beans, drained and rinsed
6 cups	arugula
1 cup	low-fat cottage cheese
Pinch	each salt and freshly ground pepper
2 cups	Basic Tomato Sauce (see recipe, page 123)
6	sheets (each 6 x 9 inches) fresh lasagna, cut in half crosswise

Béchamel Sauce:

3 tbsp	canola oil
1/4 cup	whole wheat flour
1 cup	skim milk
1 cup	chicken stock (low fat, low sodium)
1/2 cup	orange juice
1 tbsp	grated Parmesan cheese
1/4 tsp	each salt and freshly ground pepper
1/4 tsp	grated nutmeg

1. Preheat oven to 350°F.
2. In large non-stick frying pan, heat oil over medium-high heat; cook chicken, onion and garlic until browned, about 8 minutes. Add beans and mash lightly with potato masher or wooden spoon. Add arugula and cook, stirring, until wilted. Stir in cottage cheese, salt and pepper.
3. **Béchamel Sauce:** In saucepan, heat oil over medium-high heat. Add flour and cook, stirring, for 1 minute. Slowly pour in milk and stock, whisking to combine. Cook, whisking gently, until mixture is thickened, about 2 minutes. Stir in orange juice and whisk until smooth. Add Parmesan, salt, pepper and nutmeg. Remove from heat.

4. In 13- x 9-inch baking dish, spread 1 cup tomato sauce. Arrange lasagna sheets on work surface. Spoon 1/2 cup filling onto each lasagna sheet. Starting at short edge of sheet, roll up and place in baking dish, making 2 rows. Cover with remaining tomato sauce. Pour béchamel over top. Cover with foil and bake for 30 minutes. Remove foil and bake until bubbling, about 10 minutes.

Makes 6 servings.

Make Ahead: Refrigerate until cold, then cover with heavy-duty foil and freeze up to 1 month. Defrost in refrigerator. Add 15 minutes to initial baking time.

Variation: Substitute extra-lean ground beef for the chicken or turkey.

CHICKEN AND SPINACH ROTOLO

This is a novel way to use lasagna noodles. Serve with a green salad and enjoy.

12	whole wheat lasagna noodles
3 tbsp	olive oil
1	onion, chopped
2	cloves garlic, minced
8 oz	mushrooms, thinly sliced
1	green pepper, seeded and chopped
1 lb	boneless skinless chicken breasts, cut into small cubes
1	pkg (10 oz) frozen spinach, thawed and squeezed dry
1	can (28 oz) diced tomatoes
1/3 cup	skim milk
1/4 cup	light cream cheese
1/2 tsp	dried oregano
1/2 tsp	dried basil
1/4 tsp	each salt and freshly ground pepper
1 tbsp	grated Parmesan cheese
1 tsp	Splenda
1 tbsp	chopped fresh basil
1/4 cup	shredded light-style mozzarella cheese
1 tbsp	chopped fresh parsley

1. Preheat oven to 350°F.
2. In large pot of boiling salted water, cook lasagna noodles for about 10 minutes or until al dente. Drain and rinse under cold water. Lay noodles flat on damp tea towels; set aside.
3. Meanwhile, in large non-stick frying pan, heat 2 tbsp oil over medium-high heat. Cook onion, garlic, mushrooms and green pepper for about 8 minutes or until golden brown. Add chicken and cook for 5 minutes. Stir in spinach, 1 1/2 cups of the diced tomatoes, milk, cream cheese, oregano, basil, salt and pepper; cook until moisture is evaporated, 8 to 10 minutes. Transfer to large bowl and stir in Parmesan.
4. In same frying pan, heat remaining 1 tbsp oil over medium-high heat. Add

remaining tomatoes and juice, Spenda and basil. Simmer, stirring occasionally, for 15 minutes or until thickened. Spread evenly in bottom of 13- x 9-inch glass baking dish.

5. Divide chicken mixture evenly over lasagna noodles. Starting at short end, roll up each noodle and place upright on sauce in baking dish. Sprinkle with mozzarella, cover and cook for 15 minutes. Uncover and continue cooking for 5 more minutes or until cheese is melted and golden brown.

6. To serve: Place 2 rolls on plate, spoon sauce over top and sprinkle with parsley.

Makes 6 servings.

CHICKEN AND SWISS CHARD LASAGNA

There can never be too many ways to make lasagna!

1 tbsp	olive oil
4	large onions, thinly sliced
1 tsp	Splenda
1 tsp	balsamic vinegar
3/4 tsp	freshly ground pepper
1 lb	ground chicken or turkey
1	bunch Swiss chard, chopped (about 8 cups)
8 oz	mushrooms, sliced
1/2 cup	red wine
1	clove garlic, minced
1	can (28 oz) crushed tomatoes
1 tbsp	each chopped fresh rosemary and oregano (or 1 tsp dried)
1/2 tsp	salt
1 cup	low-fat cottage cheese
12	whole wheat lasagna noodles

Béchamel Sauce:

1/4 cup	canola oil
1/2 cup	whole wheat flour
4 cups	warm skim milk
2 tbsp	grated Parmesan cheese
1/4 tsp	salt
1/4 tsp	freshly ground pepper
Pinch	nutmeg

1. In non-stick frying pan, heat oil over medium-high heat. Cook onion for 10 minutes or until softened and turning golden brown. Sprinkle with Spenda; reduce heat to low and cook, stirring occasionally, for 15 minutes or until deep amber colour. Stir in vinegar and 1/4 tsp pepper. Remove from heat and set aside.
2. In large non-stick frying pan over medium heat, cook ground chicken until browned, 8 to 10 minutes. Add Swiss chard, mushrooms, red wine and garlic; cook, stirring occasionally, until mushrooms are softened, about 8 minutes.

Add tomatoes, rosemary, oregano, salt and remaining 1/2 tsp pepper; bring to boil. Reduce heat and simmer, covered, for 25 minutes. Remove from heat and stir in cottage cheese.

3. Preheat oven to 350°F.

4. **Béchamel Sauce:** In saucepan, heat oil over medium-high heat. Add flour and cook, stirring, for 1 minute. Slowly pour in milk and whisk to combine. Cook, whisking gently, until mixture is thick enough to coat back of spoon, about 5 minutes. Add Parmesan, salt, pepper and nutmeg. Remove from heat.

5. Meanwhile, in large pot of boiling water, cook lasagna noodles for about 10 minutes or until al dente. Drain and rinse under cold water. Lay noodles flat on damp tea towels; set aside.

6. Ladle 1/2 cup meat sauce into bottom of a 13- x 9-inch glass baking dish. Lay 3 noodles side by side on top of the sauce. Spread with 1/4 of the meat sauce, then 1/4 of the béchamel sauce and half of the onion. Repeat with noodles, meat sauce, béchamel sauce and onion. Repeat layers with remaining ingredients, ending with béchamel sauce. Cover dish with aluminum foil. Bake for 45 minutes, then uncover and bake for 15 minutes or until bubbly. Let cool for 10 minutes before serving.

Makes 8 servings.

BOLOGNESE PASTA SAUCE

This is a great staple sauce to have on hand. Freeze it in 1-cup portions in zip-top plastic freezer bags and place in the fridge overnight to defrost. Use in lasagna, serve with whole wheat pasta combined with cooked kidney beans, or serve over brown basmati rice.

1 tbsp	olive oil
1 lb	extra-lean ground beef
1/2 cup	skim milk
2	cloves garlic, minced
1	onion, chopped
1	red pepper, seeded and chopped
1	green pepper, seeded and chopped
1	stalk celery, chopped
1	carrot, chopped
1 tbsp	dried oregano
1 tsp	salt
1/2 tsp	freshly ground pepper
1 cup	red wine or grape juice
2	cans (28 oz each) crushed tomatoes
1 tbsp	chopped fresh basil

1. In large pot or deep frying pan, heat oil over medium-high heat. Cook beef for about 8 minutes or until browned. Pour in milk and cook for another 2 to 3 minutes or until milk is absorbed. Reduce heat to medium. Add garlic, onion, red and green peppers, celery, carrot, oregano, salt and pepper; cook, stirring, for about 5 minutes or until vegetables are softened. Pour in wine and cook, stirring and scraping up any brown bits, for about 1 minute or until wine is evaporated.
2. Add tomatoes and basil; bring to boil. Reduce heat and simmer, uncovered, for about 45 minutes or until sauce is thick and flavourful.

Makes about 6 cups.

BEEF AND BOW TIES

This recipe is a kid-pleaser. If you don't have bow tie–shaped pasta on hand, substitute any medium-size pasta.

3½ cups	whole wheat bow tie pasta
12 oz	extra-lean ground beef
1	onion, chopped
2	cloves garlic, minced
1	zucchini, chopped
1	large carrot, chopped
1	red pepper, seeded and chopped
4 oz	mushrooms, chopped
1 cup	red wine
4	medium tomatoes, chopped
1 cup	Basic Tomato Sauce (see recipe, page 123)
½ tsp	freshly ground pepper
¼ tsp	salt
¼ cup	chopped fresh parsley
2 tbsp	chopped fresh basil

1. In large pot of boiling water, cook pasta until al dente, about 10 minutes; drain and set aside.
2. In large non-stick frying pan, cook beef and onion over medium-high heat until browned, about 8 minutes. Add garlic, zucchini, carrot, red pepper and mushrooms and cook, stirring occasionally, until vegetables are softened, about 6 minutes. Add red wine and cook until liquid is evaporated.
3. Add tomatoes, tomato sauce, pepper and salt and simmer for 5 minutes. Stir in pasta, parsley and basil. Cook for 2 minutes or until warmed through.

Makes 4 to 6 servings.

PORK AND SHRIMP STIR-FRY

Stir-fries make great weeknight meals. Have Chinese-Style Pork with Hoisin Glaze (see recipe, page 194) on Sunday, and use the leftovers to make this stir-fry Monday night.

6 oz	whole wheat spaghettini
1 tbsp	canola oil
3 cups	thinly sliced cabbage
2	cloves garlic, minced
1	onion, sliced
1	red pepper, seeded and sliced
1 tbsp	minced fresh ginger
6 oz	medium raw shrimp, peeled and deveined
6 oz	leftover cooked Chinese-Style Pork (see recipe, page 194), cut into matchsticks, plus 1/3 cup leftover hoisin glaze from same recipe
1 tsp	hot chili paste
2	green onions, sliced diagonally

1. In large pot of boiling salted water, cook spaghettini for 6 minutes or until al dente. Drain and rinse with cold water. Set aside.
2. In wok or large non-stick frying pan, heat 2 tsp oil over medium-high heat. Stir-fry cabbage, garlic, onion, red pepper and ginger until tender-crisp, about 5 minutes. Transfer vegetables to bowl and set aside.
3. In same wok, heat remaining 2 tsp oil over high heat. When oil is hot, add shrimp and stir-fry until opaque, 2 to 3 minutes. Add pork and toss. Add spaghettini, vegetables, hoisin glaze and chili paste. Heat through, about 1 minute, tossing to coat mixture with sauce. Sprinkle each serving with green onions.

Makes 4 servings.

Variations:

Eliminate the noodles and serve the stir-fry over basmati rice, reducing the hoisin glaze to 1/4 cup.

Substitute firm tofu cubes for the shrimp, or double the amount of pork.

Meatless Mains

BARLEY RISOTTO WITH LEEKS, LEMON AND PEAS

Unlike traditional risotto, this barley version doesn't need to be watched and stirred continuously.

1 tbsp	olive oil
1/2 cup	chopped leek (white and light-green parts only), chopped (about 1/2 cup) (see helpful hint on page 48)
2	cloves garlic, minced
1/2 tsp	chopped fresh thyme
1 cup	barley
1/4 cup	white wine or vermouth
3 cups	chicken stock (low fat, low sodium) (and up to 1/2 cup more if needed)
1 cup	fresh or frozen and thawed peas
	Zest and juice of 1 medium lemon
2 tbsp	grated Parmesan cheese
1/4 tsp	each salt and freshly ground pepper

1. In saucepan, heat oil over medium-high heat; cook leek, garlic and thyme, stirring, for 3 minutes or until softened. Stir in barley until well coated.
2. Stir in wine until absorbed. Add stock and bring to boil. Cover and reduce heat to low; simmer, stirring occasionally, for 40 to 45 minutes or until barley is tender. If needed, stir in a little more stock or hot water near the end of cooking time to maintain a creamy consistency. Stir in peas, lemon zest and juice and Parmesan; season with salt and pepper.

Makes 4 to 6 servings.

FALAFEL WITH YOGURT-MINT SAUCE

This Middle Eastern street-food favourite is usually deep-fried. Our green-light version is lightly pan-fried in a small amount of olive oil to keep it crisp.

2	cans (19 oz each) chickpeas, drained and rinsed
4	cloves garlic, minced
3/4 cup	parsley
1 1/2 tbsp	lemon juice
1 1/2 tsp	ground cumin
1 tsp	hot pepper sauce
1 tsp	salt
3/4 cup	whole wheat flour
1/4 cup	olive oil
	Lettuce and chopped tomatoes

Yogurt-Mint Sauce:

1 cup	low-fat plain yogurt
1/2	English cucumber, grated and squeezed dry
2	cloves garlic, minced
1 tsp	dried mint
Pinch	each salt and freshly ground pepper
4	pitas, halved

1. **Yogurt-Mint Sauce:** In bowl, stir together yogurt, cucumber, garlic, mint, salt and pepper.
2. In food processor, blend together chickpeas, garlic, parsley, lemon juice, cumin, hot pepper sauce and salt. Transfer mixture to bowl and stir in flour.
3. Form mixture into 24 balls (about 2 tbsp each) and flatten slightly.
4. Heat oil in non-stick frying pan over medium-high heat. Fry falafel for 2 to 3 minutes per side or until golden brown. Serve 3 in each pita half along with lettuce, chopped tomatoes and Yogurt-Mint Sauce.

Makes 8 servings.

THAI-STYLE TOFU AND BROCCOLI

Serve hot or cold over basmati rice or whole wheat pasta.

3/4 cup	hot vegetable stock
1	stalk lemongrass, finely chopped
1 tbsp	canola oil
1 lb	firm tofu, cubed
3	cloves garlic, minced
1	hot chili pepper, seeded and finely chopped
1 tsp	toasted sesame oil
1	bunch broccoli, chopped into florets, stems peeled and chopped
1	red pepper, seeded and cut into thin strips
1/2 cup	chopped cilantro
3	green onions, chopped
2 tbsp	soy sauce
1 tbsp	lime juice

1. In small bowl, pour stock over lemongrass; set aside.
2. In wok or large non-stick frying pan, heat oil over medium-high heat. Add tofu, garlic, chili pepper and sesame oil. Stir-fry for 3 minutes or until tofu starts to turn golden. Add broccoli, red pepper and lemongrass mixture. Reduce heat to medium, cover and cook for 5 minutes. Stir in cilantro, green onions, soy sauce and lime juice; cover and cook for another 2 minutes or until broccoli is tender-crisp.

Makes 4 servings.

GRILLED PORTOBELLO MUSHROOM PIZZAS

Look for the largest mushrooms you can find. Use any favourite green-light toppings and add chopped cooked lean ham, chicken or turkey for meat lovers.

8	large portobello mushrooms, stems removed
2 tsp	olive oil
1/2 cup	Basic Tomato Sauce (see recipe, page 123) or G.I. Pesto (see recipe, page 55)
1/2 cup	light-style mozzarella cheese

Optional toppings:

Red or green peppers, seeded and chopped
Olives
Chopped fresh basil or oregano
Chopped tomatoes
Minced garlic

1. Preheat oiled grill to medium-high.
2. Brush both sides of mushrooms with oil. Grill mushrooms, stem side down, for 4 minutes. Turn and grill for another 4 minutes or until slightly softened.
3. Top mushrooms with tomato sauce and desired toppings. Sprinkle cheese over top and grill, covered, for 5 minutes or until cheese is bubbling.

Makes 4 main-course or 8 appetizer servings.

QUINOA, BEAN AND VEGETABLE CHILI

You can use any combination of beans—white, navy, pinto or chickpea—to make this chili attractive.

1 cup	quinoa, rinsed and drained
2 cups	water
1/4 tsp	salt
2 tbsp	olive oil
1 cup	chopped leeks (white and light-green parts only) (see helpful hint on page 48)
3	cloves garlic, minced
1 cup	chopped carrots
1 cup	chopped celery
1	each red and green pepper, seeded and chopped
1	hot pepper, seeded and minced
1 tbsp	chili powder
2 tsp	dried oregano
1 tsp	cocoa powder
1 tsp	ground cumin
1 tsp	Hungarian paprika
1/2 tsp	cinnamon
1/2 tsp	each salt and freshly ground pepper
2	cans (28 oz each) diced tomatoes
1	can (19 oz) black beans, drained and rinsed
1	can (19 oz) pinto beans, drained and rinsed
4	green onions, chopped
1/2 cup	low-fat sour cream

1. In frying pan over medium heat, roast quinoa for 5 minutes or until fragrant and beginning to pop. In small saucepan, bring water to boil. Add salt and roasted quinoa; cover and simmer over medium heat for 15 to 20 minutes or until water is absorbed. Remove from heat and stir. Cover and set aside.
2. Meanwhile, in large saucepan, heat oil over medium heat. Cook leeks and garlic for 5 minutes or until softened. Stir in carrots, celery, red and green peppers, hot pepper, chili powder, oregano, cocoa, cumin, paprika, cinnamon, salt and pepper. Cook for 10 minutes, stirring often. Stir in tomatoes and black

LENTIL AND TOFU STEW WITH MUSHROOMS

This stew tastes even better the next day.

1/2 cup	dried porcini mushrooms
1/4 cup	sun-dried tomatoes
1 cup	boiling water
1 cup	dried green lentils (preferably du Puy), rinsed
2 tsp	olive oil
1	onion, chopped
1/2 cup	chopped leek (white and light-green parts only) (see helpful hint on page 48)
1	clove garlic, minced
2	medium carrots, chopped
8 oz	mushrooms, sliced
14 oz	firm tofu, cubed
1 cup	vegetable stock (low fat, low sodium)
2 tbsp	tomato paste
1 tsp	dried Italian seasoning
1/2 tsp	freshly ground pepper
1/4 tsp	salt

1. Soak porcini mushrooms and sun-dried tomatoes in boiling water for 15 minutes or until softened. Reserving soaking liquid, drain; chop mushrooms and tomatoes.
2. Cook lentils in 3 cups water for 25 to 30 minutes or until soft; drain.
3. In large deep frying pan, heat oil over medium-high heat. Cook onion, leek, garlic and carrots for 10 minutes or until softened. Add mushrooms, porcini mushrooms and sun-dried tomatoes; cook for 5 minutes. Stir in tofu, lentils, reserved soaking liquid, stock, tomato paste, Italian seasoning, pepper and salt; bring to boil. Reduce heat and simmer, covered, for 20 minutes or until lentils are tender.

Makes 6 servings.

Make Ahead: Refrigerate in airtight container up to 3 days.

VEGETABLE CASSOULET

Cassoulet is a traditional French dish from the Languedoc region, consisting of beans and fatty meats such as bacon, sausage and duck. This meatless version chock full of roasted vegetables, garlic and herbs will still satisfy a hearty appetite. Make it on a weekend when you have time to savour the wonderful aromas that will fill your kitchen as it cooks. Gently reheat leftovers either in the oven or on top of the stove for a quick lunch or dinner during the week.

2 cups	dried navy beans
4	whole cloves
1	onion, halved
5 cups	chicken stock (low fat, low sodium)
4	cloves garlic, crushed
2	sprigs fresh parsley
1	sprig fresh thyme
1	bay leaf
1 cup	fresh whole-grain breadcrumbs
1 tbsp + 4 tsp	olive oil
2	carrots, sliced into 1/2-inch rounds
1	sweet potato, cut into 1-inch pieces
8 oz	celeriac (or celery root), cut into 1/2-inch pieces (about 2 cups)
2	pinches each salt and freshly ground pepper
1	onion, chopped
1	stalk celery, chopped
12 oz	Brussels sprouts (14 to 16), trimmed and halved
8 oz	mushrooms, roughly chopped
1 cup	dry white wine
1/4 cup	tomato paste
1 tbsp	chopped fresh rosemary
1 tsp	dried thyme
1 tsp	dried oregano

1. Cover beans with 6 cups water and soak for 8 hours or overnight. Drain.
2. Push 2 cloves into each onion half. Place in large saucepan along with beans, stock, garlic, parsley, thyme and bay leaf. Bring to boil; cover and

simmer for $1\frac{1}{2}$ hours or until beans are tender. Reserving cooking liquid, drain and place in large bowl. Discard onion, parsley, thyme and bay leaf.

3. Preheat oven to 425°F.

4. In bowl, toss together breadcrumbs and 1 tbsp oil. Set aside.

5. In bowl, combine carrots, sweet potato and celeriac; toss with 2 tsp oil and pinch each salt and pepper. Arrange in even layer on rimmed baking sheet and roast for 25 minutes or until golden brown but still firm. Set aside. Reduce heat to 350°F.

6. In large non-stick frying pan, heat remaining 2 tsp oil over medium-high heat. Cook onion, celery, Brussels sprouts and mushrooms, stirring occasionally, for 10 minutes or until vegetables are softened. Stir in wine, tomato paste, rosemary, thyme, oregano and pinch each salt and pepper; cook for 2 minutes. Stir into beans.

7. Spread half of the bean mixture in 16-cup casserole. Top with roasted vegetables, then rest of bean mixture. Pour in reserved cooking liquid. Bake, uncovered, for 45 minutes. Remove from oven and sprinkle breadcrumb mixture evenly over top. Return to oven and continue cooking for another 45 minutes or until topping is golden and bean mixture is bubbling.

Makes 6 to 8 servings.

Make Ahead: Cook the beans a day ahead and refrigerate. Assemble the rest of the dish the next day.

Meat Variation: Stir in $\frac{1}{2}$ lb cooked lean ham, chopped, into bean mixture in Step 6.

JOLOF RICE

This dish has its origins in Western Africa, where there are myriad variations.

2	medium Asian eggplants, sliced into 1/2-inch rounds
2 tbsp	olive oil
2	cloves garlic, minced
1	onion, chopped
1	carrot, chopped
1	green pepper, seeded and chopped
1	chili pepper, seeded and finely chopped
1 tbsp	minced fresh ginger
1/2 cup	water
2 tbsp	tomato paste
1 tbsp	white wine vinegar
2 tsp	curry powder
1 tsp	cinnamon
1/2 tsp	salt
3 cups	cooked brown basmati rice (1 cup uncooked)
1	can (19 oz) black-eyed peas
2	tomatoes, chopped

1. Place eggplant slices on baking sheet and lightly brush both sides with 1/2 tbsp oil. Broil until golden brown. Turn over slices and repeat. Set aside.
2. In large non-stick frying pan, heat remaining 1 tbsp oil over medium-high heat. Cook garlic, onion, carrot, green pepper, chili pepper and ginger until softened, about 8 minutes. Add water, tomato paste, vinegar, curry powder, cinnamon and salt. Cook, stirring, for 2 minutes. Add rice, black-eyed peas, tomatoes and eggplant, stirring until rice is warm, 2 to 3 minutes.

Makes 4 to 6 servings.

GREEN-LIGHT

GRILLED "TLT" SANDWICH

A vegetarian version of the diner classic. The longer the tofu marinates the more flavourful it will be.

2 tbsp	tomato paste
2 tbsp	apple cider vinegar
2 tbsp	soy sauce
2 tbsp	water
1	clove garlic, minced
1 tsp	Spenda
1/2 tsp	Worcestershire sauce
1	pkg (1 lb) extra-firm tofu, drained and rinsed
4	large whole wheat tortillas
4	lettuce leaves
1	tomato, sliced

1. In bowl, stir together tomato paste, vinegar, soy sauce, water, garlic, Splenda and Worcestershire sauce. Slice tofu into 1/2-inch strips and place in baking dish. Pour sauce over and toss to coat well. Cover and marinate in refrigerator for 2 hours or up to 1 day.
2. Preheat oiled grill to medium or oven to 375°F.
3. Remove tofu from marinade and grill strips for 2 minutes per side or leave in baking dish and bake for 20 minutes or until hot.
4. Divide tofu among tortillas. Top with lettuce and tomato slices and roll up.

Makes 4 servings.

BUCKWHEAT KASHA BURGERS

Serve these meatless burgers on half of a whole wheat bun dressed with your favourite green-light burger toppings or on their own with a salad.

2 cups	chicken stock or vegetable-based "chicken" stock (low fat, low sodium) (see note on page 47)
1 cup	kasha
2 tsp	olive oil
2	onions, chopped
8 oz	mushrooms, finely chopped
2	cloves garlic, minced
1/2 cup	large-flake oats, finely ground (use a spice grinder or food processor)
1 1/2 tbsp	soy sauce
1/2 tsp	freshly ground pepper

1. In saucepan, bring stock to boil. Add kasha; reduce heat and simmer for 20 minutes or until liquid is evaporated and kasha is tender. Remove from heat and let cool.
2. Meanwhile, in non-stick frying pan, heat oil over medium-high heat. Cook onion, mushrooms and garlic for 10 minutes or until softened and liquid is evaporated. Remove to large bowl. Stir in kasha, ground oats, soy sauce and pepper.
3. Using hands, form mixture into 6 patties, each about 1 inch thick. Place on non-stick griddle or in non-stick frying pan and cook for 4 to 5 minutes per side or until outside is dark brown and crisp.

Makes 6 servings.

TERIYAKI QUINOA BURGERS

These burgers are moist and packed with protein and fibre. Serve them with a simple salad or stuffed into whole wheat pita bread with tomatoes and sprouts.

1 cup	quinoa, rinsed
1/2 cup	TVP*
1	onion, finely chopped
1	clove garlic, minced
1	egg, beaten
1/4 cup	oat bran
1/4 cup	teriyaki sauce
1 tbsp	olive oil

1. In saucepan, bring 1 1/2 cups water to boil; add quinoa, reduce heat and simmer for 15 minutes or until water is absorbed.
2. Meanwhile, in large bowl, mix TVP with 1/2 cup boiling water; allow to sit for 5 minutes or until softened. Stir in cooked quinoa, onion, garlic, egg, oat bran and teriyaki sauce until well combined.
3. Using moistened hands, form mixture into eight 1/2-inch thick patties.
4. In non-stick frying pan, heat oil over medium-high heat. In batches, cook patties for 5 minutes per side or until browned and crisp.

Makes 4 servings.

* Textured Vegetable Protein (TVP) is made from dried soybean and needs to be reconstituted. It is sold in natural food stores and supermarkets under the brand name So Soya+.

Egg-free variation: To replace egg, use 1 tbsp ground flaxseed mixed with 3 tbsp warm water.

GREEN-LIGHT

MOROCCAN-SPICED VEGETABLE RAGOUT

This richly flavoured dish makes a complete meal served over brown basmati rice or whole wheat couscous. The ragout calls for garam masala, which is an Indian spice mixture that you can either buy or make using the recipe on page 119 (our version tastes much better).

1 tbsp	olive oil
1 lb	eggplant, cut into 1-inch pieces
3	cloves garlic, minced
1	large onion, sliced
2 tsp	minced fresh ginger
2 tsp	Garam Masala (see recipe, page 119)
1 tsp	paprika
1 tbsp	tomato paste
3 cups	vegetable stock
2 cups	cauliflower florets
2	carrots, cut into 1-inch pieces
1	red pepper, seeded and chopped
1	can (19 oz) chickpeas, drained and rinsed
1/2 cup	dried apricots, sliced
1/4 cup	raisins
1/2 tsp	each salt and freshly ground pepper
1/2 cup	black olives, pitted
1/4 cup	chopped cilantro

1. In large saucepan, heat oil over medium-high heat. Cook eggplant, garlic, onion, ginger, garam masala and paprika for 8 minutes or until softened. Stir in tomato paste.
2. Add stock, cauliflower, carrots, red pepper, chickpeas, apricots, raisins, salt and pepper. Cover and simmer for 15 to 20 minutes or until vegetables are tender. Stir in olives and cilantro.

Makes 4 servings.

GARAM MASALA

Use this spice mixture to add flavour to curries, soups and dips.

3	cinnamon sticks, broken
2	bay leaves
1 tbsp	green cardamom pods
1 tbsp	coriander seeds
2 tsp	black peppercorns
2 tsp	cumin seeds
2 tsp	whole cloves
2 tsp	fennel seeds
1/2 tsp	ground nutmeg

1. Place all ingredients on baking sheet and roast in 300°F oven for 10 minutes or until fragrant. Transfer to spice grinder or clean coffee grinder and grind finely.

Makes about 6 tbsp.

Make Ahead: Store in airtight container up to 6 months.

RATATOUILLE

This versatile dish can be served hot or at room temperature. It makes an excellent side dish for meat or fish, a sauce for pasta, an omelette filling, or an accompaniment for a poached egg (see page 121).

1 lb	eggplant, halved lengthwise and sliced crosswise into 1/4-inch thick rounds
1/4 cup	olive oil
	Salt and freshly ground pepper
1	Spanish onion, halved and sliced
1	red pepper, seeded and cut into 1/4-inch thick slices
1	green pepper, seeded and cut into 1/4-inch thick slices
1	medium zucchini, sliced crosswise into 1/4-inch thick rounds
3	cloves garlic, minced
1	can (28 oz) plum tomatoes, drained (reserving 1/4 cup liquid) and roughly chopped
2 tbsp	red wine vinegar
1 tbsp	chopped fresh thyme
1 tbsp	chopped fresh rosemary
2 tbsp	chopped fresh parsley
1 tbsp	chopped fresh basil

1. Place eggplant slices on a baking sheet; lightly brush both sides with 2 tbsp oil and sprinkle with salt and pepper. Broil until golden brown. Turn over slices and repeat.
2. Meanwhile, heat remaining 2 tbsp oil in heavy-bottomed, wide pot over medium-high heat. Add onion and cook until starting to turn golden, about 5 minutes. Add red and green peppers, zucchini, and salt and pepper to taste; cook, stirring occasionally, until vegetables are softened and golden brown, about 8 minutes. Add eggplant, garlic, tomatoes and reserved juice, vinegar, thyme and rosemary; simmer for 5 minutes. Stir in parsley and basil.

Makes 6 servings.

Make Ahead: Refrigerate in airtight container up to 3 days or freeze up to 3 months.

Ratatouille with Poached Egg: Scoop a small portion of ratatouille into an ovenproof dish, such as a ramekin or individual gratin dish. Make an indentation in centre of ratatouille and crack in 1 omega-3 egg. Sprinkle with salt and pepper; cover loosely with foil and place in 400°F oven for 10 to 15 minutes or until egg is set. To make several portions in a larger dish, make several indentations for eggs, cover and bake.

EGGPLANT ROLLS WITH TOMATO SAUCE

These rolls capture the flavours of the Mediterranean, and the bulgur adds fibre.

1/3 cup	olive oil
1	onion, chopped
4 oz	mushrooms, chopped
2	cloves garlic, minced
1 cup	bulgur
1/4 cup	sun-dried tomatoes, chopped
2 cups	chicken or vegetable stock (low fat, low sodium)
2	eggplants (1 1/4 lb each)
	Salt and freshly ground pepper
4 oz	chèvre (goat cheese)
4 cups	Basic Tomato Sauce (see recipe, page 123)
1/4 cup	chopped fresh basil

1. In large frying pan, heat 2 tbsp oil over medium-high heat; cook onion, mushrooms and garlic until softened, about 5 minutes.
2. Add bulgur and sun-dried tomatoes; stir until coated. Add stock and bring to boil; reduce heat and simmer, covered, for 20 minutes or until liquid is absorbed. Transfer to mixing bowl and set aside to cool.
3. Preheat oiled grill to medium.
4. Peel 2-inch wide strips of skin from opposite sides of eggplants and discard. Cut each eggplant lengthwise into 6 slices (about 1/4 inch thick). Brush both sides of slices with remaining oil; sprinkle with salt and pepper. Grill slices, turning once, until golden brown and tender, about 10 minutes. Transfer to tray and set aside.
5. Preheat oven to 375°F.
6. Stir chèvre into bulgur mixture.
7. Lay slice of eggplant on work surface and spread with 1/4 cup bulgur mixture using damp spatula. Starting at narrow end, roll up, jelly roll style. Place seam side down on tray. Repeat with remaining eggplant.
8. Pour tomato sauce into 13- x 9-inch baking dish. Place eggplant rolls on top, seam side down. Cover dish with aluminum foil and bake for 20 minutes or until sauce is bubbling. Serve 2 to 3 rolls per serving with tomato sauce and sprinkled with chopped basil.

Makes 4 to 6 servings.

BASIC TOMATO SAUCE

Freeze this sauce in 1- or 2-cup portions to have on hand for use in other recipes.

1 tbsp	olive oil
3	cloves garlic, minced
2	onions, chopped
1 cup	finely grated carrots
2	cans (28 oz each) diced tomatoes
2 tbsp	tomato paste
2 tsp	dried basil
1 tsp	dried oregano
1/2 tsp	each salt and freshly ground pepper

1. In large saucepan or deep frying pan, heat oil over medium heat. Cook garlic, onion and carrots, stirring often, for 8 minutes or until softened.
2. Add tomatoes, tomato paste, basil, oregano, salt and pepper; bring to boil. Reduce heat to medium; simmer, uncovered, for 30 minutes or until thickened slightly.

Makes about 6 cups.

Make Ahead: Refrigerate up to 1 week or freeze up to 2 months.

Variations:

Three-Mushroom Tomato Sauce: In bowl, pour in enough boiling water to cover 1 oz dried porcini mushrooms; soak for 15 minutes. Meanwhile, in frying pan, heat 2 tsp olive oil over medium heat; cook 1 cup chopped cremini and 1 cup chopped shiitake mushrooms for 5 minutes or until golden. Drain porcini, discarding soaking liquid, and stir into mushroom mixture. Stir in 2 cups Basic Tomato Sauce; simmer for 10 minutes. Toss with 3 cups cooked pasta. Makes 4 servings.

Tricolore Vegetable Tomato Sauce: In frying pan, heat 2 tsp olive oil over medium heat. Cook 1/2 each yellow and red pepper, chopped; 1/2 zucchini, chopped; and 1 cup cut green beans for 6 to 8 minutes or until vegetables are softened. Add 2 cups Basic Tomato Sauce; simmer for 10 minutes. Toss with 3 cups cooked pasta. Makes 4 servings.

Arugula and Roasted Garlic Tomato Sauce: In deep frying pan over medium heat, bring 2 cups Basic Tomato Sauce to boil. Reduce heat and stir in garlic squeezed from 1 head roasted garlic (follow instructions for roasting garlic in Mushroom Soup with Roasted Garlic and Ginger, page 46) and 1 bunch arugula, rinsed and drained. Simmer, stirring, until arugula is wilted, about 2 minutes. Toss with 3 cups cooked pasta. Sprinkle servings with 1 tsp grated Parmesan cheese or crumbled chèvre. Makes 4 servings.

SAVOURY BEANS AND APPLE

This dish was adapted from reader Nadia's recipe. Serve with brown basmati rice and a salad for a comforting vegetarian meal. Leftovers, served in whole wheat tortillas, make a tasty lunch.

1 tbsp	olive oil
1	onion, chopped
2	apples, peeled, cored and grated
2	carrots, grated
1	stalk celery, chopped
2	cloves garlic, minced
1 cup	vegetable or chicken stock (low fat, low sodium)
1/4 cup	tomato paste
2 tbsp	sherry or red wine vinegar
4 cups	cooked kidney beans (you can use canned, but it increases the G.I. rating)
2 tsp	each chopped fresh thyme and oregano
2 tsp	dried mustard
1 tsp	ground cumin
1/4 tsp	each salt and freshly ground pepper
	Low-fat sour cream or plain yogurt (optional)

1. In large, non-stick frying pan, heat oil over medium-high heat. Cook onion, apples, carrots, celery and garlic for 10 minutes or until softened.
2. In bowl, whisk together stock, tomato paste and vinegar; add to vegetable mixture in frying pan. Stir in beans, thyme, oregano, mustard, cumin, salt and pepper. Bring to boil. Reduce heat to low, cover and simmer for 45 minutes. Serve with a dollop of sour cream or yogurt, if desired.

Makes 4 to 6 servings.

How to cook dried kidney beans: In large saucepan, cover 2 cups dried kidney beans with 6 cups water and bring to boil. Remove from heat and let stand for 6 hours (or overnight). Drain, rinse and cover with another 6 cups fresh water. Bring to boil, reduce heat and simmer, partially covered, for 2 hours or until tender. Add water as needed to keep beans covered. Do not add salt while cooking, as it toughens the beans.

Fish and Seafood

DRUNKEN SALMON

Cooking the fish on cedar adds a smoky flavour, but you can also cook it directly on the barbecue. Don't worry if some of the skin sticks to the grill.

2	cloves garlic, crushed
1/2 cup	rye whisky
1/2 cup	freshly squeezed orange juice
1/3 cup	olive oil
1/4 cup	soy sauce
1 tsp	each salt and freshly ground pepper
2 lb	salmon fillet, skin on

1. Soak untreated cedar plank in water for minimum 2 hours and up to 24.
2. In 13- x 9-inch glass baking dish, whisk together garlic, whisky, orange juice, oil, soy sauce, salt and pepper. Place salmon fillet in marinade, skin side up. Cover with plastic wrap and refrigerate for 6 to 8 hours.
3. Preheat grill to medium-high.
4. Remove salmon from marinade and place on cedar plank, skin side down. Cook, with lid closed, for 10 to 13 minutes or until salmon just flakes with a fork. Be careful not to overcook.

Makes 8 servings.

MISO-CRUSTED SALMON

This recipe is a quick way to dress up salmon. Leftovers are great cold.

1	clove garlic, minced
2 tbsp	white miso
1 tbsp	tahini
2 tsp	rice vinegar
1 tsp	mirin or sweet sherry
1 lb	salmon fillet

1. Preheat oven to 425°F.
2. In small bowl, whisk together garlic, miso, tahini, vinegar and mirin.
3. Spread miso mixture evenly over surface of salmon. Bake for 10 to 12 minutes or until salmon flakes easily with a fork.

Makes 4 servings.

CITRUS-POACHED HADDOCK

Citrus fruits and fish are made for each other. This simple dish is impressive enough for company.

1	small onion, finely chopped
1	clove garlic, minced
1/4 cup	orange juice
1/4 cup	dry white wine or vermouth
1 tbsp	lemon juice
1 tsp	grated lemon zest
1/4 cup	fish, chicken or vegetable stock (low fat, low sodium)
1 lb	haddock fillet, cut into 4 pieces
2 tbsp	chopped fresh parsley or dill
1/4 tsp	each salt and freshly ground pepper

1. In large frying pan, bring onion, garlic, orange juice, wine, lemon juice and zest to boil. Boil until onion is softened and liquid is reduced by half, about 5 minutes.

2. Add stock and return to boil. Place haddock in frying pan; reduce heat and simmer gently, covered, for 10 minutes or until fish flakes easily with a fork. Using slotted spoon, remove haddock to platter and cover with foil to keep warm.

3. Bring poaching liquid to boil and reduce by one-third. Stir in parsley and season with salt and pepper. Pour sauce over fish.

Makes 4 servings.

GINGER-WASABI HALIBUT

This fish can also be cooked on the barbecue. Serve it with Cold Noodle Salad with Cucumber and Sesame (see recipe, page 75) for a refreshing summer meal.

2 tbsp	Dijon mustard
2 tsp	wasabi powder
3 tbsp	mirin or sweet sherry
2 tbsp	minced fresh ginger
2 tbsp	chopped cilantro
4	halibut pieces (4 oz each)

1. Preheat oven to 350°F.
2. In bowl, stir together mustard and wasabi powder. Stir in mirin, ginger and cilantro. Place fish in marinade and turn to coat. Let stand at room temperature for 20 minutes.
3. Place halibut on baking sheet and bake for 8 to 10 minutes or until firm to touch.

Makes 4 servings.

BRAISED PACIFIC HALIBUT

If you can find them, halibut cheeks have a beautiful dense texture and sweet flavour. You can also use haddock, tilapia or catfish in this dish.

1	pkg (10 oz) frozen chopped spinach
1 lb	Pacific halibut
1 tbsp	grainy mustard
1 tbsp	grated lemon zest
1/2 tsp	freshly ground pepper
2 tsp	olive oil
8	cloves garlic, crushed
1	onion, chopped
1/4 tsp	salt
1 cup	dry white wine

1. Preheat oven to 375°F.
2. In medium saucepan, bring 1/2 cup water to boil. Add frozen spinach, cover and cook for 2 to 3 minutes or until thawed. Drain in colander and squeeze out as much water as possible.
3. Rinse and pat fish dry with paper towel. In small bowl, stir together mustard, lemon zest and pepper. Coat fish on all sides with mixture; set aside.
4. In large ovenproof frying pan, heat oil over medium-high heat. Add garlic and onion and cook for 8 minutes or until softened. Reduce heat to medium and stir in spinach and salt. Pour in wine. Place fish on top of spinach mixture; cover and cook for 15 to 20 minutes or until fish just flakes with a fork.

Makes 4 servings.

GRILLED TUNA WITH CHIMICHURRI SAUCE

Chimichurri is traditionally served with Argentinian barbecued beef (asado), but is also delicious with grilled tuna. This recipe makes extra sauce, which can be served with poultry or meat, or stirred into hot rice.

Chimichurri Sauce:

4	cloves garlic, minced
1/2	red onion, finely chopped
1/2	red pepper, seeded and finely chopped
1/4 cup	chopped cilantro
1/4 cup	chopped fresh parsley
1 tbsp	chopped fresh oregano (or 1 tsp dried)
1/2 cup	vegetable stock
2 tbsp	extra-virgin olive oil
2 tbsp	sherry or red wine vinegar
Pinch	each salt and freshly ground pepper

4	tuna steaks, about 1/2-inch thick (4 oz each)
1/2 tsp	each salt and freshly ground pepper

1. Preheat oiled grill to medium-high.
2. **Chimichurri Sauce:** In bowl, mix together garlic, red onion, red pepper, cilantro, parsley and oregano. Stir in stock, oil, vinegar, salt and pepper.
3. Season fish with salt and pepper and grill until just charred on outside and rare in centre, about 2 minutes per side. Serve with a dollop of Chimichurri Sauce on top.

Makes 4 servings.

Make Ahead: Refrigerate sauce in airtight container up to 5 days.

BAKED STUFFED TROUT

You can use other whole fish, such as salmon, pickerel, bass or whitefish, for this dish.

1/3 cup	wild rice
2 tsp	olive oil
1	onion, chopped
1	stalk celery, chopped
4 oz	mushrooms, finely chopped
1/2 cup	chopped hazelnuts or almonds
2 tbsp	lemon juice
2 tbsp	chopped fresh parsley
Pinch	each salt and freshly ground pepper
1	whole trout, head and tail intact (about 3 lb)
1	lemon, thinly sliced
1/2 cup	white wine or vermouth

1. In large pot of boiling salted water, cook wild rice, covered, until tender, about 35 to 40 minutes. Drain and transfer to large bowl.
2. In non-stick frying pan, heat oil over medium-high heat. Cook onion, celery and mushrooms for 10 minutes or until softened. Transfer to bowl and stir in rice, hazelnuts, lemon juice, parsley, salt and pepper.
3. Preheat grill to medium-high.
4. Rinse fish well and pat dry. Fill cavity with rice stuffing. Using heavy needle and thread, sew cavity closed, or tie securely with string.
5. Place fish on piece of heavy-duty foil large enough to enclose fish. Place lemon slices along length of fish. Fold up sides of foil, pour in wine and fold over edges to seal tightly.
6. Cook on grill with lid closed for 20 to 25 minutes or until fish flakes easily with a fork.

Makes 6 servings.

Variation: Serve the fish cold with Orange-Cumin Sauce.

ORANGE-CUMIN SAUCE

This sauce also goes well with cold poached or grilled salmon.

1 cup	low-fat plain yogurt
2 tbsp	frozen orange juice concentrate
1 tsp	grated orange zest
1 tsp	ground cumin

1. In bowl, whisk together yogurt, orange juice concentrate, zest and cumin.

Makes 1 cup.

GRILLED TILAPIA WITH BLACK BEAN MANGO SALSA

The salsa in this recipe can be served with other types of fish or with grilled chicken breast.

Black Bean Mango Salsa:

1 cup	cooked black beans (see cooking instructions on page 137)
1	large ripe mango, diced
1	red pepper, seeded and finely chopped
	Zest and juice of 1 lime
3 tbsp	chopped red onion
1/4 cup	chopped fresh mint
3 tbsp	chopped cilantro
1 tbsp	extra-virgin olive oil
2 tsp	chopped fresh chili pepper or 2 tsp hot chili sauce
Pinch	each salt and freshly ground pepper

4	tilapia fillets (4 oz each)
1 tbsp	olive oil
1/2 tsp	ground cumin
1/2 tsp	each salt and freshly ground pepper
1/4 tsp	cayenne pepper

1. Preheat oiled grill to medium-high.
2. **Black Bean Mango Salsa:** In bowl, stir together black beans, mango, red pepper, lime zest and juice, red onion, mint, cilantro, oil, chili pepper, salt and pepper. Set aside.
3. Pat fillets dry using paper towel. Brush oil over both sides of fish.
4. In small bowl, mix together cumin, salt, pepper and cayenne. Rub spice mixture onto fish.
5. Place fillets on grill. Close lid and grill for about 10 minutes or until fish is opaque and flakes easily with a fork.

Makes 4 servings.

How to cook dried black beans: In large saucepan, cover 2 cups dried black beans with 6 cups water and bring to boil. Remove from heat and let stand for 6 hours (or overnight). Drain, rinse and cover with another 6 cups fresh water. Bring to boil; reduce heat and simmer, partially covered, for 1½ hours or until tender. Add water as needed to keep beans covered. Do not add salt while cooking, as it toughens the beans.

Make Ahead: Freeze beans in 1- or 2-cup amounts up to 6 months.

TOMATO AND CHEESE CATFISH

An easy weeknight dish. Serve it over pasta with a side salad.

2	medium tomatoes, chopped
1	sweet onion (such as Vidalia), chopped
1	clove garlic, minced
1	small chili pepper, seeded and minced
2 tbsp	lemon juice
1 tbsp	grated lemon zest
2 tsp	olive oil
1/4 tsp	each salt and freshly ground pepper
4	catfish fillets (4 oz each)
1/2 cup	light-style cheddar cheese

1. Preheat oven to 425°F.
2. In bowl, toss together tomatoes, onion, garlic, chili pepper, lemon juice, lemon zest, oil, salt and pepper.
3. Arrange catfish fillets in 13- x 9-inch baking dish; top with tomato mixture and sprinkle with cheese. Bake for 15 to 20 minutes or until fish flakes easily with a fork.

Makes 4 servings.

FISH TACOS

Fish tacos are a Baja, California, favourite. Here's an easy version.

1 tbsp	chili powder
1 tbsp	paprika
1/4 tsp	salt
1 lb	fish fillets (such as tilapia, snapper, haddock)
1 tsp	olive oil
1 1/2 cups	shredded cabbage
1	medium red onion, sliced
1	large carrot, shredded
1	avocado, chopped
1/4 cup	chopped cilantro
1 tbsp	lime juice
1/4 tsp	each salt and freshly ground pepper
4	large whole wheat tortillas

1. Preheat oven to 425°F.
2. In small bowl, stir together chili powder, paprika and salt. Sprinkle over fish fillets. Place on lightly oiled baking sheet and bake for 10 minutes or until fish flakes easily with a fork.
3. Meanwhile, in large bowl, toss together cabbage, onion, carrot, avocado, cilantro, lime juice, salt and pepper.
4. Flake fish into chunks and divide among tortillas. Top with cabbage mixture and roll up.

Makes 4 servings.

TUNA MUFFINS

This recipe was adapted from an idea from reader Barbara. Two of these muffins paired with a salad make a satisfying lunch or light supper.

2	slices high-fibre bread
2	cans (6 oz each) chunk light tuna, drained
1	stalk celery, chopped
1	clove garlic, minced
1/2 cup	finely chopped onion
1/3 cup	light-style cheddar cheese
2 tbsp	wheat germ or oat bran
2 tsp	dried sage
2 tsp	Worcestershire sauce
1/4 tsp	freshly ground pepper
3/4 cup	skim milk

1. Preheat oven to 350°F. Line 8 muffin tins with paper or foil liners.
2. Use food processor to make breadcrumbs from bread. Transfer to large bowl. Add tuna, celery, garlic, onion, cheese, wheat germ, sage, Worcestershire sauce and pepper. Stir in milk.
3. Divide among muffin tins, packing mixture firmly.
4. Bake for 30 minutes or until muffins are golden and crisp around edges. Run knife around edges of muffins and remove carefully from pan. Serve hot or at room temperature.

Makes 8 muffins.

Make Ahead: Wrap each muffin individually in plastic wrap and refrigerate up to 2 days or freeze in airtight container up to 1 month. Can be reheated in microwave oven.

TUNA SALAD

This mixture is also nice served in endive spears or romaine lettuce leaves.

1	can (19 oz) cannellini (white kidney) beans, drained and rinsed
1	clove garlic, minced
2	cans (6 oz each), chunk light tuna, drained
1	large tomato, chopped
1/4 cup	capers
2 tbsp	chopped fresh parsley
1 tbsp	lemon juice
1/4 tsp	each salt and freshly ground pepper
4	slices whole-grain bread

1. Using potato masher, in bowl mash half of the cannellini beans with garlic.
2. In another bowl, mix tuna, tomato, capers, parsley and lemon juice. Stir in bean mixture and salt and pepper.
3. Divide mixture evenly among bread slices.

Makes 4 to 6 servings.

BOUILLABAISSE WITH RED PEPPER ROUILLE

There is a Bouillabaisse charter that states what ingredients can be used in the traditional Marseilles fish stew. This version takes some liberties, but is hearty and tasty nonetheless. It's a great dish for entertaining.

2 tbsp	olive oil
4	cloves garlic, minced
2	onions, chopped
2	stalks celery, chopped
1	medium carrot, chopped
1 cup	chopped leeks, (white and light-green parts only) (see helpful hint on page 48)
1/2	fennel bulb, chopped
3/4 cup	white wine
3	plum tomatoes, chopped
2 tbsp	Pernod or Sambuca
1 tbsp	tomato paste
2	bay leaves
1	sprig fresh thyme
1	1-inch thick strip orange zest
1 tsp	saffron threads, crumbled
1 tsp	salt
1/2 tsp	freshly ground pepper
6 cups	fish stock or chicken stock (low fat, low sodium)
36	mussels, scrubbed and beards removed
24	clams, scrubbed
10 oz	Mediterranean firm-fleshed fish (such as red snapper, rock fish, red mullet or striped bass) cut in chunks
1/2 lb	large raw shrimp, peeled and deveined
1/4 cup	chopped fresh parsley

Red Pepper Rouille:

1	roasted red pepper, seeded and peeled
2	slices whole wheat bread, torn in pieces, crusts removed
2	cloves garlic, minced
Pinch	each salt and freshly ground pepper
1/3 cup	extra-virgin olive oil

1. In large Dutch oven, heat oil over medium heat; cook garlic, onions, celery, carrots, leeks and fennel until softened, about 8 minutes. Stir in wine, tomatoes, Pernod, tomato paste, bay leaves, thyme, orange zest, saffron, salt and pepper; cook for 2 minutes. Add stock; bring to boil. Simmer, uncovered, for 30 minutes or until level is slightly reduced.

2. **Red Pepper Rouille:** Meanwhile, in blender or food processor, purée roasted red pepper, bread, garlic, salt and pepper. With machine running, in a thin steady stream, pour in oil until creamy. If too thick, thin with a little warm water.

3. Add mussels, clams (discarding any with cracked shells or that do not open when tapped) and fish to pot, stirring gently; cover and cook for 5 minutes. Add shrimp and cook for 5 minutes or until fish is opaque, shrimp are pink, and mussels and clams have opened.

4. Discard any unopened mussels and clams. Gently stir in parsley. Using slotted spoon, divide fish and seafood evenly among warmed bowls. Ladle broth and vegetables over, and serve drizzled with a spoonful of rouille.

Makes 6 servings.

MUSSELS PROVENÇAL

Serve this easy but elegant dish, full of the flavours of southern France, with a simple green salad.

4 lb	mussels
1 tbsp	olive oil
1/2 cup	chopped shallots
4	cloves garlic, minced
1	can (28 oz) plum tomatoes, drained and chopped
2 tsp	fennel seeds
1 1/2 cups	dry white wine
1/2 tsp	each salt and freshly ground pepper
1/4 cup	chopped fresh parsley

1. Scrub mussels under running water; trim off any beards. Discard any with cracked shells and any that do not close when tapped. Set aside.
2. In Dutch oven or large heavy saucepan, heat oil over medium-high heat. Cook shallots and garlic for 5 minutes or until softened. Add tomotoes and fennel seeds; cook for 5 minutes. Stir in wine, salt and pepper; bring to boil.
3. Add mussels and cook, covered, for 5 minutes or until mussels open. Discard any unopened mussels. Serve in large bowls, sprinkled with parsley.

Makes 4 servings.

CORNMEAL-MUSTARD SCALLOPS WITH SPINACH AND BEANS

A delightful combination of texture and flavour.

1/4 cup	grainy mustard
1/3 cup	cornmeal
1 lb	sea scallops
2 tsp	olive oil
1/3 cup	chicken stock
1	can (14 oz) soy beans or cannellini (white kidney) beans, drained and rinsed
2	cloves garlic, minced
1	bag (10 oz) baby spinach
1 tbsp	lemon juice
Pinch	each salt and freshly ground pepper

1. Preheat oven to 200°F.
2. In bowl, combine mustard and cornmeal.
3. Pat scallops dry using paper towels. Add scallops to cornmeal mixture, tossing to coat well on all sides.
4. In large non-stick frying pan, heat oil over medium-high heat. Sear scallops on all sides, turning carefully, until coating is golden and crisp. Remove to plate; cover and place in oven to keep warm. Leave any remaining cornmeal coating in frying pan.
5. In same frying pan, add stock, beans and garlic. Cook, stirring, for 2 minutes. Add spinach and cook, stirring, for 3 minutes or until spinach is wilted. Stir in lemon juice, salt and pepper. Divide spinach mixture among plates and top with scallops.

Makes 4 servings.

CHILI-LIME SHRIMP

Perfect summer backyard barbecue fare.

1/4 cup	lime juice
2	hot chili peppers, seeded and diced
1 tbsp	grated lime zest
1 tbsp	olive oil
2 tsp	chili powder
1 lb	shell-on raw jumbo shrimp
	Lime wedges

1. Preheat oiled grill to medium-high.
2. In large bowl, whisk together lime juice, chili peppers, lime zest, oil and chili powder. Stir in shrimp, tossing to coat. Marinate at room temperature for 30 minutes, tossing occasionally.
3. Grill for 3 minutes per side or until shells are pink. Serve with lime wedges.

Makes 4 servings.

STIR-FRIED SHRIMP IN BLACK BEAN SAUCE

Serve this stir-fry over rice or whole wheat or cellophane noodles. If you can't find a Napa cabbage, use regular green cabbage.

1/4 cup	chicken stock (low fat, low sodium) or water
3 tbsp	black bean sauce
1 tbsp	hoisin sauce
1 tsp	cornstarch
1 tsp	sesame oil
1	clove garlic, minced
1 tbsp	canola oil
2	stalks celery, chopped
1	red pepper, seeded and chopped
6 oz	shiitake mushrooms, stemmed and sliced
4 cups	shredded Napa cabbage
1 lb	raw shrimp, peeled and deveined
3	green onions, sliced on the diagonal
1/4 cup	chopped cilantro

1. In small bowl, whisk together stock, black bean sauce, hoisin, cornstarch, sesame oil and garlic.
2. In wok or large non-stick frying pan, heat canola oil over medium-high heat. Stir-fry celery, red pepper, mushrooms and Napa cabbage for about 5 minutes or until cabbage is tender-crisp.
3. Add shrimp, green onions and stock mixture; stir-fry until shrimp are opaque and sauce is thickened, about 3 minutes. Sprinkle with cilantro.

Makes 4 servings.

SPICY SAUTÉED CALAMARI WITH BEANS, TOMATOES AND OLIVES

This makes a nice summer lunch served on a bed of arugula or spinach. Cooking the calamari quickly over high heat keeps it tender.

1 lb	cleaned calamari
3	cloves garlic, minced
1 tbsp	lemon juice
1 tsp	hot chili paste
1/4 tsp	salt
1/2 tsp	freshly ground pepper
1	can (19 oz) cannellini (white kidney) beans, drained and rinsed
1	tomato, chopped
1/2 cup	pitted black olives
2 tsp	olive oil
1/4 cup	roughly chopped fresh parsley

1. Using sharp knife, lightly score calamari in criss-cross pattern, being careful not to cut all the way through flesh.
2. In bowl, whisk together garlic, lemon juice, chili paste, salt and pepper. Add beans, tomato, olives and parsley; toss to coat.
3. In non-stick frying pan, heat oil over high heat. Add calamari and cook for 2 minutes or until just opaque. Add bean mixture, toss to combine and heat through, about 1 minute.

Makes 4 servings.

Poultry

CHICKEN TAGINE

This Moroccan-inspired stew's flavour develops with time. Make it on the weekend and reheat it for a satisfying Monday night meal. Serve on a bed of basmati rice.

3	cloves garlic, minced
2 tsp	minced fresh ginger
1 tsp	paprika
1 tsp	ground cumin
1/2 tsp	cinnamon
1/2 tsp	turmeric
1/2 tsp	freshly ground pepper
1/4 tsp	saffron, crumbled
1/4 tsp	salt
4	boneless skinless chicken breasts, halved lengthwise
2 tsp	olive oil
1	large onion, thinly sliced
2 cups	water
1	can (19 oz) chickpeas, drained and rinsed
1/2 cup	dried apricots, sliced
1/4 cup	raisins
1/4 cup	chopped cilantro
1/4 cup	chopped fresh parsley
1/2	lemon, thinly sliced
2 tbsp	lemon juice
1/4 cup	chopped fresh mint

1. In large bowl, combine garlic, ginger, paprika, cumin, cinnamon, turmeric, pepper, saffron and salt. Add chicken and combine well, rubbing spice mixture into meat. Set aside.
2. In large deep non-stick frying pan, heat oil over medium-high heat. Add onion and cook until softened, about 5 minutes. Add chicken and brown on all sides, about 5 minutes. Add water, chickpeas, apricots, raisins, cilantro, parsley, lemon and lemon juice ; bring to boil. Reduce heat, cover and cook for 30 minutes or until chicken is no longer pink inside. Sprinkle with chopped mint.

Makes 4 servings.

WHITE CHICKEN CHILI

This is a quick one-pot meal, perfect for the weekday rush.

2 tsp	olive oil
4 cups	shredded cabbage
3	cloves garlic, minced
2	onions, chopped
1	carrot, chopped
1	jalapeño pepper, minced (optional)
1 lb	boneless skinless chicken breasts, cubed
2 1/2 cups	chicken stock (low fat, low sodium)
1	can (19 oz) cannellini (white kidney) beans, drained and rinsed
2 tsp	ground cumin
1 tsp	chili powder
1 tsp	dried oregano
1/4 tsp	salt

Optional toppings:

Salsa, no added sugar
Chopped cilantro
Non-fat sour cream or low-fat plain yogurt

1. In deep frying pan or Dutch oven, heat oil over medium-high heat. Cook cabbage, garlic, onion, carrot and jalapeño pepper, if using, for 10 minutes or until softened, stirring occasionally. Push vegetables to side of pan; add chicken and cook for 3 minutes. Stir in stock, beans, cumin, chili powder, oregano and salt. Cook for 15 to 20 minutes or until chicken is no longer pink inside.
2. Serve with any of the optional toppings over cooked basmati rice, if desired.

Makes 4 to 6 servings.

CHICKEN RICE CASSEROLE

This comforting casserole can be prepared in the morning and popped into the oven when you come home from work.

2 tsp	olive oil
1 lb	ground chicken
1	large sweet onion (such as Vidalia)
1	clove garlic, minced
2 tsp	dried Italian seasoning (or mixture of dried rosemary, thyme, basil and oregano)
1 tsp	salt
1/2 tsp	freshly ground pepper
1 cup	chicken stock (low fat, low sodium) or water
1	can (28 oz) crushed tomatoes (or 1 can tomatoes, puréed)
3/4 cup	brown basmati rice
6 cups	chopped broccoli (florets and stems)

1. Preheat oven to 350°F.
2. In large non-stick frying pan over medium-high heat, cook ground chicken, onion and garlic until browned, about 8 minutes. Add Italian seasoning, salt and pepper; cook for another 5 minutes. Stir in stock, crushed tomatoes and rice.
3. Pour mixture into large ovenproof casserole dish; stir in broccoli. Cover and bake for 1 hour or until rice is tender.

Makes 4 to 6 servings.

Helpful Hint: To save time, you can use frozen broccoli florets.

Make Ahead: Freeze up to 1 month. Defrost in refrigerator and reheat in microwave. Or place frozen portion in saucepan with a little water; reheat over medium heat, stirring often.

CHICKEN SANDWICH WITH ROASTED RED PEPPER AND ONION CONFIT

Roasting your own peppers is easy, but you can also use jarred roasted red peppers to save time.

1 tbsp	olive oil
2	large sweet onions (such as Vidalia), thinly sliced
2 tbsp	balsamic vinegar
1 tsp	Splenda
Pinch	each salt and freshly ground pepper
1	red pepper
3 cups	shredded cooked chicken (or 12 oz sliced deli chicken breast)
4	slices toasted whole wheat high-fibre bread
4	slices light-style Swiss cheese

1. Preheat oven to 425°F.
2. In non-stick frying pan, heat oil over high heat. Cook onion until turning golden, about 5 minutes. Reduce heat to medium-low and cook for 20 minutes or until onion is very soft and deep golden brown. Stir in vinegar, Spenda, salt and pepper; cook for 5 minutes. Cover and keep warm.
3. Char red pepper on all sides over gas flame or under broiler until blackened on all sides. Place in bag; let stand for 10 minutes. Pull skin off and discard seeds and membrane. Cut into strips.
4. Divide chicken among slices of bread. Top with red pepper, onion and slice of cheese. Place on baking sheet and bake until cheese is melted, about 5 minutes.

Makes 4 servings.

HOISIN CHICKEN PARCELS

These little packages can be made in no time.

1/4 cup	hoisin sauce
2 tbsp	soy sauce
1 tbsp	mirin or sherry
1	clove garlic, minced
1 tbsp	minced fresh ginger
1 tsp	sesame oil
2	boneless skinless chicken breasts, cut crosswise into 1/2-inch slices
1 cup	snow peas
1	red pepper, seeded and thinly sliced
2	green onions, chopped

1. Preheat oiled grill to medium-high or oven to 425°F.
2. In large bowl, combine hoisin sauce, soy sauce, mirin, garlic, ginger and sesame oil. Add chicken, snow peas, red pepper and green onions; toss to coat.
3. Divide mixture between two 12- x 14-inch pieces of aluminum foil. Fold up packages and seal tightly. Grill over medium-high heat, or cook in oven, for 15 to 20 minutes or until chicken is cooked through and vegetables are tender-crisp.

Makes 2 servings.

CHICKEN FINGERS WITH APRICOT-MUSTARD DIPPING SAUCE

Pair these chicken fingers with some crunchy raw veggies for a family-friendly meal.

2	egg whites
2 tbsp	soy sauce
1	clove garlic, minced
1 lb	boneless skinless chicken breasts, cut into 1/2-inch strips
1/2 cup	toasted sesame seeds
2 tsp	canola oil

Apricot-Mustard Dipping Sauce:

1/4 cup	all-fruit apricot preserves (no sugar added)
1/4 cup	water
1 tbsp	Dijon mustard

1. Preheat oven to 375°F.
2. In bowl, whisk together egg whites, soy sauce and garlic. Add chicken and toss to coat. Cover and refrigerate for at least 1 hour or up to 1 day.
3. Remove chicken from marinade, allowing excess to drip off. Sprinkle all sides with sesame seeds and place on baking sheet brushed with oil. Bake for 5 minutes per side or until chicken is no longer pink inside.
4. Dipping Sauce: Meanwhile, in small bowl, stir together preserves, water and mustard. Serve with chicken fingers.

Makes 4 servings.

CHICKEN BHUNA

This wonderful Indian dish has been adapted from a recipe from reader Ros. Make lots and freeze any left over for another day. Serve with basmati rice and a salad.

2 tsp	olive oil
2	cloves garlic, chopped
1	onion, chopped
1	red or yellow pepper, seeded and chopped
1/2 cup	chopped celery
1 tsp	minced fresh ginger
1 tsp	cinnamon
1/2 tsp	each ground cumin and turmeric
1/4 tsp	each ground allspice and cloves
1/4 tsp	each salt and freshly ground pepper
2 tbsp	tomato paste
1 lb	boneless skinless chicken breasts or thighs, cut into bite-size cubes
1 cup	chicken stock (low fat, low sodium)
1	can (14 oz) diced tomatoes
1 cup	bulgur
1/4 cup	chopped cilantro

1. In large deep non-stick frying pan, heat oil over medium-high heat. Cook garlic, onion, red pepper and celery for 5 minutes or until softened. Add ginger, cinnamon, cumin, turmeric, allspice, cloves, salt and pepper. Cook, stirring constantly, for 2 minutes. Stir in tomato paste.
2. Add chicken and cook, stirring, for 3 minutes or until outside of chicken is no longer pink. Stir in stock, tomatoes and bulgur. Bring to boil. Cover and simmer for 30 minutes or until bulgur is cooked and chicken is no longer pink inside. Stir in cilantro.

Makes 4 servings.

BASQUE CHICKEN

This stew contains rich flavours reminiscent of Spanish regional cooking. It's a great dish for entertaining, and can be made up to a day ahead and reheated.

1 tbsp + 2 tsp	olive oil
2 lb	skinless chicken breasts and thighs
1/4 tsp	each salt and freshly ground pepper
6 oz	Italian-style chicken or turkey sausage, cut into 1/2-inch slices
3	cloves garlic, sliced
2	onions, roughly chopped
2	peppers (any colour), cut into 1-inch pieces
3/4 cup	brown basmati rice
1	can (28 oz) tomatoes, drained and quartered
1	can (19 oz) cannellini (white kidney) beans, drained and rinsed
1 cup	chicken stock
1/2 cup	dry white wine
2 tbsp	tomato paste
1 tbsp	chopped mixed fresh herbs (choose from rosemary, oregano, thyme and marjoram)
1 tsp	paprika, preferably smoked
1/2 cup	olives
1/4	large orange, unpeeled, cut into 4 pieces

1. Preheat oven to 350°F.
2. In large, deep, ovenproof frying pan, heat 1 tbsp oil over high heat. Sprinkle chicken with salt and pepper. Brown on all sides. Remove to plate. Add remaining 2 tsp oil, sausage, garlic, onions and peppers. Cook for 5 minutes or until onion is golden brown. Stir in rice, tossing to coat. Stir in tomatoes, beans, stock, wine, tomato paste, herbs and paprika.
3. Place chicken on top of mixture. Scatter olives and orange over top. Cover and bring to simmer on top of stove. Place in oven and bake for 1 hour or until chicken and rice are cooked.

Makes 6 to 8 servings.

CHICKEN SATAYS

These skewers are delicious hot or at room temperature. They also make a popular party appetizer.

2	cloves garlic, minced
2 tbsp	soy sauce
2 tbsp	frozen apple juice concentrate
1 tbsp	teriyaki sauce
2 tsp	peanut or almond butter
1 tsp	tahini
1/2 tsp	sesame oil
1 lb	boneless skinless chicken breasts, cut into 1/2-inch strips

1. In bowl, stir together garlic, soy sauce, apple juice concentrate, teriyaki sauce, peanut butter, tahini and sesame oil. Add chicken and toss to coat thoroughly with mixture. Cover and marinate in refrigerator for at least 1 hour or up to 1 day.
2. Preheat oiled grill to medium-high.
3. Remove chicken from marinade and thread onto bamboo skewers that have been soaked for 30 minutes. Grill for 2 minutes per side or until no longer pink inside.

Makes about 16 satays.

CHICKEN STIR-FRY WITH BROCCOLI

This quick chicken stir-fry will get everyone eating their broccoli. You can use other vegetables that you have on hand too.

1	egg white
1 tsp	Chinese Spice Mix (see recipe, page 195), optional
1 lb	boneless skinless chicken breast, cut into bite-size pieces
3 tbsp	orange juice
2 tbsp	soy sauce
1 tbsp	hoisin sauce
1 tbsp	oyster sauce
2 tsp	cornstarch
1 tsp	sesame oil
1 tbsp	canola oil
2	cloves garlic, minced
1	onion, thinly sliced
1	red pepper, seeded and sliced
1 tbsp	minced fresh ginger
1	bunch broccoli, trimmed and cut into 1-inch pieces
1/4 cup	water
1 cup	bean sprouts
1/2 cup	coarsely chopped cashews

1. In medium bowl, whisk together egg white and spice mix, if using. Add chicken and toss to coat well. Set aside.
2. In small bowl, stir together orange juice, soy sauce, hoisin sauce, oyster sauce, cornstarch and sesame oil until smooth. Set aside.
3. In wok or large non-stick frying pan, heat canola oil over high heat. Add chicken mixture and stir-fry for 5 minutes or until almost cooked through. Remove to plate or bowl.
4. Add garlic, onion, red pepper and ginger. Stir-fry for 1 minute. Add broccoli and water and bring to boil. Cover and cook for 5 minutes or just until broccoli is tender-crisp.
5. Add chicken and sauce. Stir-fry for 3 minutes or until sauce is thickened and chicken is cooked through. Stir in bean sprouts and cashews.

Makes 4 servings.

ZESTY BARBECUED CHICKEN

The marinade in this recipe helps keep the breasts moist when they are cooked.

1/4 cup	lemon juice
2 tsp	chopped fresh rosemary
2 tsp	canola oil
4	boneless skinless chicken breasts
1/3 cup	Zesty Barbecue Sauce (see below)

1. In bowl, whisk together lemon juice, rosemary and oil. Add chicken breasts; toss to coat. Marinate at room temperature for 30 minutes.
2. Preheat oiled grill to medium-high.
3. Remove chicken from marinade and brush with Zesty Barbecue Sauce; grill for 6 minutes. Turn, brush with more sauce and grill for another 6 minutes or until chicken is no longer pink inside.

Makes 4 servings.

ZESTY BARBECUE SAUCE

This sauce will keep up to 2 weeks if refrigerated in an airtight container.

1	can (14 oz) tomato sauce
2	cloves garlic, minced
1/4 cup	frozen apple juice concentrate
1/4 cup	tomato paste
2 tbsp	cider vinegar
1 tbsp	each Splenda and Dijon mustard
2 tsp	chili powder
1/2 tsp	Worcestershire sauce
1/4 tsp	each salt and freshly ground pepper

1. In large saucepan, combine tomato sauce, garlic, apple juice concentrate, tomato paste, vinegar, Splenda, mustard, chili powder, Worcestershire sauce, salt and pepper; bring to boil. Reduce heat and simmer for about 20 minutes or until reduced and thickened.

Makes about 1 1/2 cups.

CHICKEN PEPERONATA

Serve this easy dish with rice or pasta.

4	skinless chicken breasts
2 tbsp	whole wheat flour
1 tbsp	olive oil
2	cloves garlic, minced
1	onion, sliced
1	each red, yellow and green pepper, seeded and thinly sliced
1	can (28 oz) chopped tomatoes
1/2 cup	chopped sun-dried tomatoes
1 tbsp	chopped fresh oregano (or 1 tsp dried)
1/4 tsp	each salt and freshly ground pepper

1. Dredge chicken breasts in flour. In large non-stick frying pan, heat oil over medium-high heat. Add chicken and brown on both sides; remove to plate.
2. Add garlic and onion to frying pan and cook until softened, about 5 minutes. Add peppers, chopped tomatoes, sun-dried tomatoes, oregano, salt and pepper; bring to boil. Place chicken on top of mixture; reduce heat and cook, covered, for 15 to 20 minutes or until chicken is no longer pink inside.

Makes 4 servings.

Make Ahead: Wrap well and freeze up to 1 month. Defrost in refrigerator overnight and reheat gently on stovetop.

CHICKEN TIKKA

This recipe uses garam masala, an Indian spice mixture with myriad uses. You can buy it, but our version on page 119 is far superior.

1/2 cup	Yogurt Cheese (see recipe, page 248)
2	cloves garlic, minced
1 tbsp	minced fresh ginger
2 tsp	lemon juice
1 tsp	salt
1/2 tsp	ground cumin
1/2 tsp	chili powder
1/2 tsp	Garam Masala (see recipe, page 119)
1/4 tsp	turmeric
1 lb	boneless skinless chicken breasts, cut into bite-size cubes

1. In bowl, stir together Yogurt Cheese, garlic, ginger, lemon juice, salt, cumin, chili powder, garam masala and turmeric. Add chicken and toss to coat thoroughly with mixture. Cover and marinate in refrigerator for 4 to 6 hours.
2. Preheat oiled grill to medium-high or oven to 400°F.
3. Remove chicken from marinade and thread onto 4 bamboo skewers that have been soaked for 30 minutes.
4. Grill, turning occasionally, until chicken is no longer pink inside, about 10 minutes, or place on baking sheet and bake for 10 to 12 minutes.

Makes 4 servings.

CHICKEN SCHNITZEL

Kids love this dish. You can substitute more traditional veal scallopini or leg cutlet for the chicken.

4	boneless skinless chicken breasts
1/2 cup	whole wheat flour
1/2 tsp	each salt and freshly ground pepper
2	egg whites
1/2 cup	wheat bran
1/4 cup	wheat germ
1/4 cup	fine dry whole wheat breadcrumbs
1 tsp	grated orange zest
1 tbsp	olive oil
1/2 cup	orange juice
1/2 cup	chicken stock (low fat, low sodium)
1/2 cup	thinly sliced dried apricots
1/4 cup	chopped green onion

1. Using meat mallet or rolling pin, pound chicken breasts between 2 pieces of plastic wrap until about 1/4 inch thick.
2. In large shallow dish or pie plate, combine flour, salt and pepper. In another shallow dish or pie plate, whisk egg whites. In third dish or pie plate, combine wheat bran, wheat germ, breadcrumbs and orange zest.
3. Pat chicken dry and dredge in flour mixture, shaking off excess. Dip in egg whites, letting excess drip off, then dredge in wheat bran mixture, coating completely.
4. In large non-stick frying pan, heat oil over medium-high heat. Fry chicken (in batches if necessary) for 4 minutes per side or until golden brown and just cooked through. Transfer schnitzel to platter and place in 200°F oven to keep warm.
5. In same frying pan, combine orange juice, stock and apricots. Bring to boil and allow to reduce until slightly thickened and syrupy, about 3 minutes. Stir in green onion. Pour sauce over schnitzel.

Makes 4 servings.

SPICY ROASTED CHICKEN WITH TOMATOES AND TARRAGON

This recipe is from our friend Meryle. Serve it with basmati rice or quinoa to soak up the sauce.

4 cups	cherry or grape tomatoes, halved
5	cloves garlic, crushed
1/4 cup	olive oil
2 tbsp	chopped fresh tarragon
2 tsp	red pepper flakes
4	boneless skinless chicken breasts
1 tsp	each salt and freshly ground pepper

1. Preheat oven to 450°F.
2. In large bowl, toss tomatoes with garlic, oil, 1 tbsp tarragon, and red pepper flakes.
3. Place chicken on rimmed baking sheet. Arrange tomato mixture in single layer around chicken. Sprinkle with salt and pepper. Roast for 30 to 35 minutes or until chicken is no longer pink inside. Transfer chicken to platter. Spoon tomatoes and juices over. Sprinkle with remaining tarragon.

Makes 4 servings.

COFFEE- AND SPICE-RUBBED CHICKEN BREASTS

You can make a large batch of the rub, minus the coffee, and keep it in an airtight container up to 3 months. When you're ready to use it, just add the coffee.

4	chicken breast halves (about 1 lb)
2	cloves garlic, minced
1 tbsp	freshly ground coffee
1 tsp	paprika
1 tsp	ground cumin
1/2 tsp	chili powder
1/2 tsp	ground coriander
1/4 tsp	cinnamon
1/8 tsp	ground cloves
1/4 tsp	each salt and freshly ground pepper
1 tbsp	olive oil

1. Preheat oiled grill to medium-high.
2. Using meat mallet or rolling pin, pound chicken breasts between 2 pieces of plastic wrap until about 1/2 inch thick.
3. In small bowl, mix together garlic, coffee, paprika, cumin, chili powder, coriander, cinnamon, cloves, salt and pepper. Stir in oil to make smooth paste. Rub mixture evenly into both sides of chicken breasts.
4. Grill chicken until no longer pink inside, 3 to 4 minutes per side.

Makes 4 servings.

Make Ahead: After coating with rub, chicken can be wrapped and refrigerated up to 4 hours before cooking.

SPINACH-STUFFED CHICKEN BREASTS

Oats are an unlikely ingredient in a savoury sauce but work well here as a thickener and an extra hit of fibre.

2 tbsp	olive oil
2	onions, chopped
1	clove garlic, minced
2 cups	chopped fresh spinach
1 tbsp	chopped fresh mint leaves
1/2 tsp	each salt and freshly ground pepper
4	chicken breast halves
1/4 cup	extra low-fat soft cheese (such as Boursin)
1 tbsp	grated Parmesan cheese
1	roasted red pepper, seeded, peeled and cut into strips
1	can (28 oz) diced tomatoes
1/2 cup	white wine
1/2 cup	chicken stock
1/4 tsp	crumbled saffron strands
1/2 cup	large-flake oats

1. In large non-stick frying pan, heat 1 tbsp oil over medium-high heat. Cook half the onion, and garlic until softened, about 5 minutes. Add spinach; cook, stirring, until wilted, about 2 minutes. Stir in mint and 1/4 tsp each salt and pepper. Transfer to bowl and set aside to cool.
2. Meanwhile, using meat mallet or rolling pin, pound chicken breasts between 2 pieces of waxed paper until 1/4 inch thick.
3. Add soft cheese and Parmesan to spinach mixture and stir to combine. Divide mixture among chicken breasts and spread evenly, almost to edges. Lay strips of roasted red pepper over top. Starting from short edge, roll up chicken breasts and seal, placing seam side down on cutting board. Sprinkle with remaining salt and pepper.
4. Heat remaining 1 tbsp oil in large non-stick frying pan over medium-high heat. Cook remaining onion until softened, about 5 minutes. Add tomatoes, wine, stock and saffron; simmer, covered, for 8 minutes. Stir in oats. Arrange

chicken rolls on top of sauce and continue to simmer, covered, for 20 to 25 minutes or until chicken is cooked through.

5. To serve, place chicken on plate and spoon sauce around and over top.

Makes 4 servings.

TURKEY-QUINOA LOAF

Quinoa adds extra protein and fibre to this meat loaf. Serve it with Cranberry-Orange Sauce (page 171). Leftovers are great cold.

1/2 cup	quinoa, rinsed and drained
Pinch	salt
12 oz	ground turkey or chicken
1	apple, peeled and grated (about 1 cup)
1	onion, finely chopped
1	clove garlic, minced
1/4 cup	green onion, chopped
2 tbsp	finely chopped fresh sage
1 tsp	Worcestershire sauce
1 tsp	salt
1/2 tsp	freshly ground pepper
1/4 tsp	ground allspice
1/4 tsp	ground cloves

1. Preheat oven to 350°F.
2. In frying pan over medium heat, toast quinoa for 5 minutes or until fragrant and beginning to pop. In small saucepan, bring 1 cup water and pinch salt to boil. Add toasted quinoa; cover and simmer over medium heat for 15 to 20 minutes or until water is absorbed. Set aside.
3. In large bowl, mix together turkey, apple, onion, garlic, green onion, sage, Worcestershire sauce, salt, pepper, allspice and cloves. Add quinoa and mix thoroughly. Pack mixture into 8- x 4-inch loaf pan. Bake for 1 hour or until meat thermometer registers 160°F when inserted in centre of meat loaf.

Makes 6 servings.

Make-Ahead: Meat loaf can be prepared up to 1 day ahead, and then baked.

Muffin Variation: Place mixture in 12 muffin tins and bake for about 30 minutes or until meat thermometer registers 160°F when inserted in centre of muffin.

TURKEY SAUSAGE WITH CABBAGE AND BARLEY

You can find good chicken and turkey sausages in the supermarket. Just check the ingredients to make sure they don't contain a lot of added fillers or sugar.

1 tbsp	olive oil
1 lb	turkey or chicken sausages, cut into 1/2-inch rounds
6 cups	shredded cabbage
1	onion, sliced
1	clove garlic, minced
1/2 tsp	caraway seeds
2 cups	chicken stock (low fat, low sodium)
1 tbsp	cider vinegar
1 tbsp	grainy mustard
3/4 cup	barley

1. In deep non-stick frying pan, heat oil over medium-high heat. Add sausage and brown on all sides, about 5 minutes. Add cabbage, onion, garlic and caraway seeds; cook, stirring, until cabbage has wilted slightly, about 3 minutes.
2. In bowl, whisk together stock, vinegar and mustard. Add to frying pan along with barley; stir. Bring to simmer; cover and cook, stirring occasionally and adding more water if too dry, for 40 minutes or until barley is tender.

Makes 4 servings.

FRUIT- AND NUT-STUFFED TURKEY BREAST

This is a festive green-light alternative to the traditional holiday bird. Serve it with vegetables and Cranberry-Orange Sauce (see recipe, page 171).

1 tbsp	olive oil
1	onion, chopped
1	clove garlic, chopped
1/2 cup	cubed whole wheat bread
1/4 cup	chopped dried apples
1/4 cup	chopped dried cranberries
1/4 cup	pistachios, roughly chopped
2 tsp	chopped fresh thyme
1 tsp	dried sage
1/4 tsp	pepper
1 1/4 cup	chicken stock (low fat, low sodium)
1	boneless skinless turkey breast (about 2 lb)
2 tsp	olive oil
1/4 tsp	each salt and freshly ground pepper
1/2 cup	apple cider or juice
1 tbsp	cornstarch
1 tbsp	water

1. Preheat oven to 325°F.
2. In non-stick frying pan, heat oil over medium-high heat. Cook onion and garlic for 5 minutes or until softened. Stir in bread, apples, cranberries, pistachios, thyme, sage and pepper. Pour in 1/4 cup of stock and stir until absorbed. Remove from heat and set aside.
3. Using chef's knife, cut along edge of one side of the turkey breast. Continue to slice in half almost all the way through. Open meat like a book and, using meat mallet, pound turkey to flatten slightly.
4. Spread stuffing mixture evenly over one half of the breast. Fold other half over stuffing and, using kitchen string, tie breast at evenly spaced intervals to fully enclose stuffing in breast. Rub with oil and sprinkle with salt and pepper. Place turkey on rack set in small roasting pan. Roast for 45 minutes. Remove pan from oven and pour in remaining 1 cup stock. Roast for another 30 minutes or until meat thermometer inserted in centre

of turkey reaches 180°F. Transfer to cutting board; tent with foil and let stand for 15 minutes.

5. Meanwhile, place roasting pan over medium heat. Stir in apple cider and bring to boil, scraping up any brown bits from bottom of pan. In small bowl, whisk together cornstarch and water. Whisk into stock mixture and boil, stirring, for 1 minute or until thickened slightly and glossy.

6. Slice turkey into 1/2-inch thick slices. Spoon sauce over top.

Makes 6 to 8 servings.

CRANBERRY-ORANGE SAUCE

GREEN-LIGHT

As well as being a festive accompaniment for turkey, this sauce pairs well with grilled pork and chicken.

1 1/2 cups	fresh or frozen cranberries
1/4 cup	dried cranberries
1/4 cup	Splenda
1/4 cup	fresh orange juice
2 tbsp	Grand Marnier or any orange-flavoured liqueur (optional)
1 tbsp	frozen orange juice concentrate
1 tbsp	grated orange zest
1/2 tsp	cinnamon

1. In saucepan, combine cranberries, dried cranberries, Splenda, orange juice, Grand Marnier, if using, orange juice concentrate, orange zest and cinnamon; bring to boil. Reduce heat to simmer and cook, stirring occasionally, for 10 minutes or until cranberries burst and sauce thickens.

Makes about 1 1/2 cups.

Make Ahead: Refrigerate up to 1 week.

Meat

BLUEBERRY BEEF BURGERS

Blueberries help make these burgers moist and juicy.

1/2 cup	fresh or frozen and thawed wild blueberries
2	cloves garlic, minced
1 tbsp	balsamic vinegar
1 tbsp	Dijon mustard
1 tsp	Worcestershire sauce
1/2 tsp	salt
1/4 tsp	freshly ground pepper
1/2 cup	ground flaxseed
1/4 cup	rolled oats
1 lb	extra-lean ground beef
2	whole wheat buns
4	lettuce leaves
4	tomato slices

1. Preheat oiled grill or broiler to medium-high.
2. Place blueberries in bowl of food processor. Add garlic, vinegar, mustard, Worcestershire sauce, salt and pepper; purée. Scrape into large bowl. Stir in flaxseed and oats. Add ground beef and mix with hands or wooden spoon until well combined.
3. Form meat mixture into 4 patties, each about 1/2 inch thick. Place on grill or broiler pan and cook, turning once, until no longer pink inside, 4 to 5 minutes per side. Serve each patty on half a whole wheat bun. Top with lettuce and tomato slices.

Makes 4 servings.

STUFFED PEPPERS

Here's a twist on a classic comfort dish.

12 oz	extra-lean ground beef
2	cloves garlic, minced
1	onion, chopped
1	omega-3 egg
3/4 cup	barley
2 tbsp	tomato paste
1/2 tsp	each salt and freshly ground pepper
4	large peppers (any colour)
2 cups	Basic Tomato Sauce (see recipe, page 123)

1. In bowl, mix together beef, garlic, onion, egg, barley, tomato paste, salt and pepper.
2. Cut top off each pepper and remove seeds and ribs. Pack each with beef mixture. Place in large saucepan and add enough water to just cover top of peppers. (Don't worry if they turn on their sides during cooking; the filling will stay put.) Bring to boil; reduce heat and simmer for 45 minutes or until barley is tender. Remove peppers from water and place on serving platter. Heat tomato sauce and pour over peppers before serving.

Makes 4 servings.

Make Ahead: Peppers can be prepared up to 1 day ahead; cover and refrigerate. Or wrap well and freeze up to 1 month. Microwave from frozen, or thaw in refrigerator and reheat in oven. Pour hot tomato sauce over reheated peppers.

BEEF STROGANOFF

You can make this dish early in the day and reheat just before serving. Serve with boiled new potatoes or whole wheat pasta.

1 lb	top round steak, cut into strips
1/2 tsp	each salt and freshly ground pepper
1 tbsp	olive oil
1 tbsp	non-hydrogenated margarine
1/2 cup	chopped shallots
8 oz	mushrooms, sliced
1 cup	beef broth (low fat, low sodium)
1 tbsp	tomato paste
1 tsp	Worcestershire sauce
1 tsp	dried mustard
3/4 cup	non-fat sour cream

1. Sprinkle steak strips with salt and pepper. In large non-stick frying pan, heat oil over high heat. Add meat in single layer (working in batches if necessary) and cook until just brown on outside, about 1 minute per side. Remove meat to plate and set aside.
2. In same frying pan, melt margarine over medium-high heat. Add shallots and cook until starting to soften, about 2 minutes. Add mushrooms and cook until tender and all liquid is evaporated, 8 to 10 minutes.
3. In small bowl, whisk together beef broth, tomato paste, Worcestershire sauce and mustard. Return steak to pan and pour broth mixture over. Simmer until liquid reduces and thickens slightly, about 12 minutes. Add sour cream and cook on low heat until heated through.

Makes 4 servings.

STEAK AND PEPPER SIZZLE

Marinate the beef in the morning (or the night before) and come home to a quick and easy dinner.

2	cloves garlic, minced
1/2 cup	red wine
1 1/2 tbsp	tomato paste
1 tbsp	Dijon mustard
1 tsp	Worcestershire sauce
1/2 tsp	freshly ground pepper
1/4 tsp	salt
1 lb	top round steak, trimmed of all visible fat and thinly sliced
1 tbsp	olive oil
2	onions, sliced
1	each red and green pepper, seeded and sliced

1. In bowl, whisk together garlic, red wine, tomato paste, mustard, Worcestershire sauce, pepper and salt. Add beef, stirring to coat. Cover and marinate in refrigerator for at least 6 hours or up to 24.
2. In large non-stick frying pan, heat oil over medium-high heat. Cook onions and red and green peppers for 8 minutes or until tender-crisp. Remove to plate and cover to keep warm.
3. Add steak and marinade to frying pan; cook for 5 minutes or until steak is browned and cooked to desired doneness.
4. Return vegetables to frying pan and toss with meat and sauce until well combined.

Makes 4 servings.

MARINATED FLANK STEAK

Serve this at your next summer barbecue party, paired with a big green salad.

1/4 cup	soy sauce
1/4 cup	orange juice
3 tbsp	canola oil
3 tbsp	rice vinegar
2	cloves garlic, minced
2 tbsp	minced fresh ginger
1 tbsp	Dijon mustard
1 lb	flank steak

1. In shallow dish, whisk together soy sauce, orange juice, oil, vinegar, garlic, ginger and mustard. Add flank steak and turn to coat evenly. Cover and marinate in refrigerator for at least 4 hours or up to 8 hours, turning meat occasionally.
2. Preheat oiled grill to medium-high.
3. Discarding marinade, place steak on grill; close lid and cook, turning once, for about 8 minutes per side for medium-rare or until desired doneness. Transfer to cutting board and tent with foil; let stand for 5 minutes, then slice thinly across the grain.

Makes 4 servings.

BEEF CUTLETS IN MUSHROOM GRAVY

An updated version of old-fashioned Salisbury steak. The beef stays moist and juicy while cooking in the beefy gravy. Serve with new potatoes and green beans for a comforting supper.

1	omega-3 egg
2	cloves garlic, minced
1/3 cup	crushed whole wheat crackers
1/3 cup	chopped black or green olives
1/2 cup	grated carrot
1 tsp	Worcestershire sauce
1/4 tsp	salt
1/2 tsp	freshly ground pepper
12 oz	extra-lean ground beef
2 tsp	olive oil
1	large onion, sliced
8 oz	mushrooms, sliced
2 cups	beef broth (low fat, low sodium)
1 tbsp	tomato paste

1. In large bowl, whisk egg. Add garlic, crackers, olives, carrot, Worcestershire sauce, salt and pepper; stir to combine. Add ground beef and combine well, using hands to distribute ingredients evenly.
2. Preheat oiled grill to medium-high.
3. Form meat mixture into 4 oval patties, each about 3/4 inch thick. Place on grill or in non-stick frying pan and cook until browned, 3 to 4 minutes per side.
4. Meanwhile, heat oil in large non-stick frying pan over medium-high heat. Cook onion and mushrooms until softened and turning golden, about 8 minutes. Stir in broth and tomato paste; bring to boil. Add beef cutlets, cover and simmer for 10 minutes or until beef is no longer pink inside.

Makes 4 servings.

COCONUT CURRY BEEF

Just a little bit of peanut butter and light coconut milk make this curry taste rich and creamy.

3 tbsp	orange juice
2 tbsp	fish sauce
2 tsp	cornstarch
2 tsp	soy sauce
1 lb	top round steak, cut into strips
2 tsp	canola oil
1	onion, chopped
1	clove garlic, minced
1/2 tsp	yellow curry paste (or to taste)
1/2 cup	light coconut milk
1 tbsp	100% peanut butter
1 tbsp	lime juice
2 tsp	Splenda
1/4 cup	chopped cilantro
2 tbsp	unsalted peanuts, chopped

1. In bowl, whisk together orange juice, fish sauce, cornstarch and soy sauce. Stir in beef, tossing to coat. Marinate at room temperature for 30 minutes or refrigerate for up to 1 day.

2. In large non-stick frying pan, heat oil over medium-high heat. Cook onion and garlic for 5 minutes or until softened. Add curry paste and cook for 1 minute. Add beef and cook for 2 minutes or until browned but still pink inside. Stir in coconut milk, peanut butter, lime juice and Splenda. Cook, tossing to coat meat with sauce, for another 2 minutes. Garnish with cilantro and peanuts.

Makes 4 servings.

Chicken Tikka, page 162
This recipe uses garam masala, an Indian spice mixture with myriad uses.

Blanquette de Veau, page 182
A classic French bistro dish to warm you up on a cold winter's night.

Roasted Pork Tenderloin with Balsamic Glaze and Gingered Peach Salsa, page 192
This is delicious accompanied by basmati rice, asparagus and a side salad.

Roasted Green Bean, Tomato and Shiitake Fricassee, page 201
This colourful side dish goes well with a simple grilled breast of chicken.

Oatmeal Buttermilk Pancakes, page 213
Make pancake breakfasts a weekend tradition.
Serve them with fresh fruit or applesauce.

Blueberry Rock Cakes, page 235
You can substitute any berry in this; just adjust the amount of sugar substitute accordingly.

Apple Upside-Down Cake, page 262
This cake is just as good made with pears.

One-Bowl Chocolate Cake with Ganache Icing, page 266
To make a layered birthday cake, cut this cake in half and spread ganache between the layers before icing the top and sides. The cake can also be enjoyed without the Ganache.

COCOA SPICE–RUBBED GRILLED STEAK

Slicing the steak thinly makes the recommended portion of steak appear more substantial. Serve it atop a simple green salad or sautéed vegetables and rice.

2 tbsp	Cocoa Spice Rub (see below)
1 tbsp	olive oil
1	clove garlic, minced
8 oz	top sirloin grilling steak

1. Preheat oiled grill to medium-high.
2. In bowl, stir together Cocoa Spice Rub, oil and garlic. Rub mixture into all sides of steak. Grill steak for about 4 minutes per side or until medium-rare inside. Slice steak thinly and serve.

Makes 2 servings.

COCOA SPICE RUB

In Phase II, rub two 6-oz T-bone steaks with this spice mixture.

2 tbsp	cocoa powder
2 tsp	turmeric
1 tsp	ground cumin
1 tsp	ground coriander
1 tsp	ground allspice
1 tsp	ground cardamom
1/2 tsp	each salt and freshly ground pepper

1. In small bowl, mix together all ingredients.

Makes about 1/3 cup.

Make Ahead: Keep in airtight container up to 6 months.

BLANQUETTE DE VEAU

A classic French bistro dish to warm you up on a cold winter's night.

2 tbsp	olive oil
1 lb	lean boneless veal shoulder, cut into 1-inch pieces
3 cups	chicken stock (low fat, low sodium)
1/2 cup	dry white wine
1	carrot, halved and sliced crosswise into 1/2-inch pieces
1	stalk celery, chopped
1	clove garlic, minced
2 tsp	chopped fresh thyme
1	bay leaf
10 oz	pearl onions, peeled (see helpful hint on page 183)
1 tbsp	non-hydrogenated margarine
6 oz	small mushrooms, quartered
1 tbsp	lemon juice
2 tbsp	cornstarch
1/2 cup	low-fat plain yogurt
2 tbsp	chopped fresh parsley
1/4 tsp	each salt and freshly ground pepper

1. In large heavy saucepan, heat 1 tbsp oil over medium-high heat. Lightly brown veal on all sides. Add 2 cups stock, wine, carrot, celery, garlic, thyme and bay leaf. Bring to simmer and cook, covered, for 20 minutes or until veal is tender.
2. Meanwhile, in small frying pan, cook onions in remaining 1 cup stock, covered, for 15 minutes or until onions are tender and stock is absorbed. Remove from heat and set aside.
3. In non-stick frying pan, heat remaining 1 tbsp oil and margarine over medium-high heat. Cook mushrooms for 5 minutes or until softened. Stir in lemon juice. Remove from heat and set aside.
4. Using slotted spoon, remove veal and vegetables from broth to bowl. Discard bay leaf. In small bowl, blend cornstarch with 3 tbsp broth; whisk back into broth in saucepan and cook, stirring, over medium-high heat until thickened and smooth. Stir in yogurt. Return veal and vegetables to pot

along with reserved pearl onions and mushrooms. Stir in parsley, salt and pepper.

Makes 4 servings.

Helpful Hint: To peel pearl onions, cover them with boiling water; let stand for 2 minutes. Plunge into cold water and slip off skins.

GRILLED VEAL ROLLS

Double this recipe when entertaining. The rolls can be made up to 1 day ahead and grilled just before serving.

1	zucchini
1 tbsp	olive oil
1/2 cup	pitted black olives
2 tbsp	tomato paste
1	clove garlic, minced
1 lb	veal, cut into 4 slices and pounded thin, or 4 leg cutlets
4	very thin slices lean prosciutto

1. Preheat oiled grill to medium-high.
2. Slice zucchini lengthwise into 1/4-inch strips. Brush with 1 tsp oil and grill for 3 to 4 minutes per side or until golden and tender. Do not turn off grill.
3. In food processor, purée olives, tomato paste, garlic and remaining oil.
4. Lay veal flat on work surface. Divide olive purée among veal slices, spreading evenly over meat. Top each with slice of prosciutto and slice of zucchini. Starting at short end, roll up veal, jelly-roll style, and secure with a toothpick.
5. Grill for 8 minutes, turning once, or until browned but still slightly pink inside.

Makes 4 servings.

GINGER-CITRUS VEAL KABOBS

We don't often think of veal for kabobs, but when combined with orange and ginger, it makes a wonderful, tangy summer dish.

3	cloves garlic, minced
1/2 cup	orange juice
1/4 cup	white wine or vermouth
2 tbsp	olive oil
2 tbsp	minced fresh ginger
1 tbsp	grated orange zest
1 tbsp	chopped fresh rosemary
1/4 tsp	freshly ground pepper
1 lb	veal sirloin or shank, cut into 1-inch cubes
12	oyster mushrooms
12	cherry tomatoes
1	red pepper, seeded and cut into chunks

1. In large bowl, whisk together garlic, orange juice, wine, oil, ginger, orange zest, rosemary and pepper. Add veal, stirring to coat. Cover and marinate in refrigerator for 1 hour or up to 12 hours.
2. Preheat oiled grill to medium-high.
3. Thread veal, mushrooms, tomatoes and red pepper onto 4 metal or soaked wooden skewers. Place on grill; close lid and cook, turning occasionally, for 10 minutes or until browned but still pink inside.

Makes 4 servings.

OSSO BUCO WITH CAMPARI AND ORANGE GREMOLATA

Make an Italian-themed dinner: start with a green salad, serve this osso buco for the entrée and have Panna Cotta with Blueberry Sauce (see recipe, page 254) for dessert. Finish off with a decaf cappuccino—buon appetito!

6	pieces meaty veal shank osso buco (6 to 8 oz each)
1/2 tsp	each salt and freshly ground pepper
2 tbsp	whole wheat flour
3 tbsp	olive oil
3	cloves garlic, minced
1	onion, chopped
3/4 cup	chopped carrot
3/4 cup	chopped celery
3	sprigs fresh parsley
2	sprigs fresh thyme
3/4 cup	dry white wine
1/4 cup	Campari
1	can (28 oz) plum tomatoes, coarsely chopped, with juice
1 cup	beef stock (low fat, low sodium)
1/4	orange (with peel)
2	bay leaves

Gremolata:

1/4 cup	chopped fresh parsley
1	clove garlic, minced
2 tsp	finely grated orange zest

1. Preheat oven to 350°F.
2. Season shanks with salt and pepper. Place flour on plate and dredge shanks in flour, coating all sides and shaking off excess flour.
3. In ovenproof pot large enough to hold meat in single layer, heat 1 tbsp oil over medium-high heat. In 2 batches, brown shanks well on all sides. Transfer to plate.
4. Reduce heat to medium and add remaining 2 tbsp oil to pot along with garlic, onion, carrot, celery, parsley and thyme. Cook, stirring, until onion is golden and vegetables are starting to soften, about 10 minutes. Add wine and

Campari, stirring to loosen brown bits on bottom of pan. Add tomatoes, stock, orange and bay leaves. Arrange shanks in pot in single layer and bring to simmer. Cover pot and braise in centre of oven, basting every 20 minutes and turning once, for 2 hours or until meat is very tender when pierced with a fork.

5. **Gremolata:** Meanwhile, in small bowl, stir together parsley, garlic and orange zest. Set aside.

6. Remove shanks from pot, place on a plate and cover with foil to keep warm. Return the pot with the braising liquid to stovetop and remove bay leaves, parsley and thyme. If necessary, bring liquid to boil and reduce a little to concentrate flavour.

7. Place portion of veal on each plate or shallow bowl. Ladle braising liquid and vegetables over. Sprinkle with Gremolata.

Makes 6 servings.

Make Ahead: Cover and refrigerate Gremolata up to 3 hours.

Saffron Risotto: The traditional accompaniment to osso buco is saffron risotto. To make a G.I. version, use the Barley Risotto recipe, page 100, with the following changes: Omit the lemon and peas. Substitute 1 onion, chopped, for the leek and add 1/4 tsp crumbled saffron threads to stock.

ELK MEDALLIONS WITH CRANBERRY-BALSAMIC SAUCE

Elk and venison are rich, flavourful steaks, so a little goes a long way. Because they are so lean, be careful not to overcook them. Both are buttery tender when cooked medium-rare but quickly turn leathery when well done.

1 cup	beef stock (low fat, low sodium)
1 tbsp	Dijon mustard
1 tbsp	balsamic vinegar
1 tbsp	chopped fresh thyme (or 1 tsp dried)
1	clove garlic, minced
1 tsp	Worcestershire sauce
1/4 tsp	freshly ground pepper
4	elk or venison medallions (4 oz each)
1/4 cup	dried cranberries

1. In large bowl, whisk together 1/2 cup stock, mustard, vinegar, thyme, garlic, Worcestershire sauce and pepper. Add elk, stirring to coat. Cover and marinate in refrigerator for at least 4 hours or up to 24 hours.
2. Preheat oiled grill to medium-high.
3. Reserving marinade, remove meat. Grill for 3 to 4 minutes per side or until no more than medium doneness. Remove to plate and cover to keep warm.
4. In non-stick frying pan, bring reserved marinade and remaining 1/2 cup stock to boil. Add dried cranberries and simmer sauce until slightly thickened and reduced by half, about 3 minutes. Serve sauce over elk.

Makes 4 servings.

LAMB CHOPS WITH MINT PESTO CRUST

Serve with peas and new potatoes for a lovely spring supper.

1 cup	tightly packed mint leaves, finely chopped
3	cloves garlic, minced
1/4 cup	finely chopped almonds
1 tbsp	balsamic vinegar
1/4 tsp	each salt and freshly ground pepper
3 tbsp	olive oil
1 lb	lean lamb loin chops, visible fat removed

1. Preheat oiled grill to medium-high.
2. In blender or food processor, purée mint, garlic, almonds, vinegar, salt and pepper until smooth. With motor running, pour in oil in steady stream.
3. Brush both sides of lamb chops with pesto. Grill chops for 5 minutes per side for medium-rare.

Makes 4 servings.

SPEEDY PORK AND LENTILS

You can put this meal together in less than 30 minutes. Celeriac (or celery root) is an underused vegetable that here complements the pork and lentils.

1 cup	lentils
3 cups	water
1	lemon wedge
1	celeriac, peeled and cut into 1/2-inch chunks
1 tbsp	olive oil
1 tsp	chopped fresh thyme
Pinch	each salt and freshly ground pepper
1	onion, chopped
1	clove garlic, minced
12 oz	pork tenderloin, cut into strips
1/2 cup	dry Marsala or red wine
1 tbsp	Dijon mustard

1. Preheat oven to 425°F.
2. Place lentils, water and lemon in medium pot. Bring to boil and simmer for 20 minutes or until tender. Drain and return to pot; discard lemon wedge.
3. Meanwhile, place celeriac on rimmed baking sheet and toss with 1 tsp oil, thyme, salt and pepper. Bake for 15 minutes or until just tender. Add to pot with lentils and keep warm.
4. Heat remaining 2 tsp oil in non-stick frying pan over medium-high heat. Cook onion and garlic for 5 minutes or until softened. Add pork and cook for 2 to 3 minutes or until pork is browned but still pink inside. Stir in Marsala and mustard and bring to boil. Reduce heat slightly and cook for 2 minutes or until sauce is thickened slightly. Serve over lentils and celeriac.

Makes 4 servings.

PORK CHOPS WITH PEARS AND GINGER

You can substitute apples for the pears if you'd like.

4	boneless pork loin chops, trimmed of fat
1/2 tsp	each salt and freshly ground pepper
2 tsp	olive oil
2	Bosc pears, cored and cut into eighths
1 cup	sliced leeks (white and light-green parts only) (see helpful hint on page 48)
1 tbsp	minced fresh ginger
1 tsp	Splenda
1 cup	chicken stock (low sodium, low fat)
2 tbsp	apple cider vinegar

1. Sprinkle pork chops on both sides with salt and pepper. In non-stick frying pan, heat oil over medium-high heat. Add chops and cook for 3 to 4 minutes per side or until slight hint of pink remains in centre. Remove to plate.
2. Add pears, leeks and ginger to frying pan. Sprinkle with Splenda. Cook, stirring frequently, until leek is softened and pears are turning golden. Pour in stock and vinegar. Allow to simmer for 5 minutes or until pears are softened and sauce is reduced slightly. Return pork and any accumulated juices to frying pan. Simmer for 2 minutes or until pork is heated through.

Makes 4 servings.

ROASTED PORK TENDERLOIN WITH BALSAMIC GLAZE AND GINGERED PEACH SALSA

This is delicious accompanied by basmati rice, asparagus and a side salad.

Gingered Peach Salsa:

3	medium peaches, peeled and chopped
1	clove garlic, minced
1/2 cup	finely chopped red pepper
1/4 cup	finely chopped green onion
2 tbsp	lime juice
2 tbsp	chopped fresh cilantro
1 tbsp	minced fresh ginger
1/2 tsp	salt

1/2 cup	balsamic vinegar
1 lb	pork tenderloin
2 tsp	olive oil
1/2 tsp	each salt and freshly ground pepper

1. **Gingered Peach Salsa:** In bowl, stir together peaches, garlic, red pepper, green onion, lime juice, cilantro, ginger, and salt. Set aside, refrigerating until needed.
2. Preheat oven to 400°F.
3. In saucepan, bring vinegar to simmer and allow to reduce by half or until thickened and syrupy. Set aside.
4. Using sharp knife, trim any excess fat and silverskin from tenderloin. Rub pork all over with oil and sprinkle with salt and pepper. In ovenproof frying pan over high heat, brown tenderloin on all sides. Remove from heat and brush tenderloin with reduced vinegar. Place frying pan in oven for about 10 to 15 minutes or until meat thermometer reaches 155°F or pork has only a hint of pink inside. Let stand for 5 minutes before slicing. Serve with Gingered Peach Salsa.

Makes 4 servings.

Make Ahead: Refrigerate Gingered Peach Salsa, covered, up to 6 hours.

PORK MEDALLIONS DIJON

Eating the green-light way doesn't mean you have to sacrifice flavour. This pork is fork tender, and the tasty sauce is rich and creamy.

2	pork tenderloins (about 12 oz each)
5 tbsp	whole wheat flour
3/4 tsp	each salt and freshly ground pepper
2 tbsp	olive oil
2	onions, thinly sliced (about 2 cups)
1	clove garlic, minced
1/4 cup	Dijon mustard
1 1/4 cups	skim milk
1/2 cup	dry white wine
1 tbsp	chopped fresh tarragon

1. Slice pork into 3/4-inch medallions. Place between 2 pieces of waxed paper; using meat mallet or rolling pin, pound to about 1/4-inch thickness.
2. On dinner plate, combine 3 tbsp flour and 1/2 tsp each salt and pepper; dredge pork. In large non-stick frying pan, heat 1 tbsp oil over medium-high heat. Cook pork until golden brown on both sides, 5 to 7 minutes; remove to plate.
3. In same frying pan, heat remaining 1 tbsp oil over medium heat. Cook onions and garlic, stirring often, for 5 minutes or until softened. Reduce heat to medium-low; cook, stirring occasionally, for 10 minutes or until golden. Add remaining 2 tbsp flour and stir to coat onion. Add mustard; cook for 2 minutes. Stir in milk, wine and remaining 1/4 tsp each salt and pepper. Cook, stirring constantly, until thickened. If mixture is too thick, stir in 1 tbsp warm water. Stir in tarragon. Return pork to pan and cook until heated through, about 1 minute.

Makes 6 servings.

CHINESE-STYLE PORK WITH HOISIN GLAZE

This is such a versatile recipe; serve two people this and save the rest to make either the Pork and Shrimp Stir-Fry (see recipe, page 98) or a delicious sandwich by wrapping sliced glazed pork and shredded lettuce or spinach in a whole wheat tortilla.

1	pork tenderloin (about 1 lb)
1	clove garlic, minced
1/4 cup	soy sauce
1/4 cup	hoisin sauce
1 tbsp	Splenda or honey
1 tbsp	mirin or dry sherry
1 tsp	sesame oil
1 tsp	Chinese Spice Mix (see page 195)
1 tsp	canola oil
2/3 cup	chicken stock (low fat, low sodium)

1. Carefully cut small slits all over pork to ensure marinade penetrates meat. In medium bowl, whisk together garlic, soy sauce, hoisin sauce, Splenda, mirin, sesame oil and Chinese Spice Mix. Add pork to marinade and rub all over to coat well. Cover and refrigerate for 24 hours, turning pork a few times as it marinates.
2. Preheat oven to 375°F.
3. Remove pork from marinade, wiping off any excess. Reserve marinade. Heat frying pan over high heat. Add canola oil and swirl to coat pan. Add pork and sear until golden brown on all sides, about 2 minutes. Remove pork to rack set in shallow roasting pan. Roast pork in top third of oven for 15 minutes or until meat thermometer registers 140°F when inserted in centre of tenderloin.
4. In small saucepan, combine reserved marinade and stock. Bring to boil over medium-high heat. Reduce heat and simmer gently until mixture is reduced to a syrupy consistency, 6 to 8 minutes.
5. To serve, slice pork thinly and drizzle with glaze.

Makes 4 to 6 servings.

Make Ahead: Leftovers can be wrapped well and refrigerated up to 3 days. Glaze can be refrigerated in an airtight container up to 3 days.

CHINESE SPICE MIX

Use this spice mix to perk up sautéed vegetables, stir into low-fat yogurt or mayonnaise to use as a veggie dip, or add to ground beef or chicken when making hamburgers.

10	whole cloves
10	cardamom pods
1 tsp	coriander seeds
1 tsp	fennel seeds
1 tsp	cumin seeds
1/2 tsp	peppercorns
1/2 tsp	ground ginger
1/4 tsp	cinnamon
1/4 tsp	turmeric

1. In dry frying pan over low heat, toast cloves, cardamom, coriander, fennel, cumin seeds and peppercorns, stirring frequently, for 5 minutes or until spices are fragrant and starting to pop. (Be careful not to burn.) Stir in ginger, cinnamon and turmeric. Transfer to spice grinder and grind finely.

Makes about 2 tbsp.

Make Ahead: Store in airtight container up to 3 months.

Vegetables and Side Dishes

BRAISED CARROTS AND PEPPERS

A different but simple way to serve vegetables.

2 tsp	olive oil
1 lb	carrots (about 4 medium), peeled and cut into 1/2-inch thick slices
1	red or yellow pepper, seeded and cut into 1/2-inch wide strips
1	red onion, sliced into 1/2 inch wide strips
1	clove garlic, minced
1/4 tsp	each salt and freshly ground pepper
1/2 cup	chicken broth (low salt, low sodium)
1 tbsp	orange juice

1. In large non-stick frying pan, heat oil over medium-high heat. Add carrots, red pepper, onion, garlic, salt and pepper; toss to coat with oil.
2. Arrange in even layer in pan and cook for 5 minutes or until bottoms of vegetables are browned. Turn and cook for another 4 minutes to brown other side.
3. Pour in chicken broth; cover and simmer for 3 minutes or until liquid is almost evaporated. Remove lid, add orange juice and toss to coat vegetables.

Makes 4 servings.

GRILLED ASPARAGUS WITH SAFFRON MAYONNAISE

This dish is an excellent addition at a barbecue buffet. Serve the mayonnaise as a dip for any other grilled vegetables, or as a sandwich spread.

2 lb	asparagus
2 tsp	olive oil
Pinch	each salt and freshly ground pepper

Saffron Mayonnaise:

1/4 cup	low-fat plain yogurt
1/4 cup	low-fat mayonnaise
2 tbsp	red wine vinegar
1	clove garlic, minced
1/4 tsp	saffron threads, crumbled
1/4 tsp	each salt and freshly ground pepper

1. Preheat oiled grill to medium-high.
2. Snap tough ends off asparagus spears and discard. Toss asparagus with oil and sprinkle with salt and pepper. Grill, turning occasionally, until asparagus is tender-crisp, 8 to 10 minutes.
3. **Saffron Mayonnaise:** In bowl, stir together yogurt, mayonnaise, vinegar, garlic, saffron, salt and pepper.
4. To serve, arrange warm or room temperature asparagus on platter with bowl of mayonnaise on the side for dipping.

Makes 6 servings.

Make Ahead: Asparagus can be made up to 1 day ahead. Refrigerate Saffron Mayonnaise in airtight container up to 5 days.

MEDITERRANEAN OVEN-ROASTED TOMATOES

These tomatoes are a wonderful accompaniment to grilled fish or meat. They are also great for lunch paired with some lean ham, cottage cheese and a slice of high-fibre whole-grain bread.

4	large tomatoes
3	anchovy fillets, chopped
2 tbsp	olive oil
1	clove garlic, minced
1 tbsp	Dijon mustard
1 tbsp	balsamic vinegar
1/4 tsp	freshly ground pepper
2 tbsp	chopped fresh basil

1. Preheat oven to 400°F.
2. Slice tomatoes in half horizontally and place, cut side up, in shallow baking dish.
3. In small bowl, whisk together anchovies, oil, garlic, mustard, vinegar and pepper. Spoon evenly over tomatoes. Bake for 25 to 30 minutes or until tomatoes are very soft and wrinkled.
4. Sprinkle basil over top of tomatoes.

Makes 4 servings.

ROASTED GREEN BEAN, TOMATO AND SHIITAKE FRICASSEE

This colourful side dish goes well with a simple grilled breast of chicken.

1 lb	green beans, trimmed
2	medium tomatoes, cut into eighths
1/4 cup	olive oil
1/4 tsp	each salt and freshly ground pepper
2	cloves garlic, finely chopped
1	red onion, chopped
8 oz	shiitake mushrooms, stemmed and sliced
1 tbsp	freshly squeezed lemon juice
1/2 cup	dry white wine or vermouth
1 tbsp	chopped fresh basil

1. Preheat oven to 400°F. Arrange green beans and tomatoes on baking sheet. Drizzle with 2 tsp oil and toss to coat. Sprinkle with salt and pepper. Roast for 10 to 12 minutes or just until tender.
2. Meanwhile, in frying pan, heat remaining oil over medium-high heat. Add garlic and onion; cook for 1 minute. Add mushrooms; cook until soft and golden, 5 to 7 minutes.
3. Add lemon juice, then pour in wine and cook until wine is absorbed, 2 to 3 minutes. Add green beans, tomatoes and basil; toss.

Makes 4 servings.

LEMONY STIR-FRIED VEGETABLES

The lemon really enhances the flavour of this easy vegetable dish.

2 tsp	canola oil
10	shiitake mushrooms, stemmed and sliced
2	carrots, thinly sliced on the diagonal
1	red, yellow, green or orange pepper, sliced
1	zucchini, halved lengthwise and sliced on the diagonal
1 tbsp	minced fresh ginger
1	clove garlic, minced
2 cups	snow peas, trimmed
4	green onions, sliced on the diagonal
	Zest and juice of 1 lemon
1 tbsp	soy sauce
1/4 cup	toasted sesame seeds

1. In wok or large non-stick frying pan, heat oil over medium-high heat. Add mushrooms, carrots, red pepper, zucchini, ginger and garlic. Stir-fry for 2 to 3 minutes.
2. Add snow peas and green onions. Stir-fry for another 2 to 3 minutes or until vegetables are tender-crisp.
3. Stir in lemon zest and juice and soy sauce. Cook for 1 minute. Sprinkle in sesame seeds, tossing to coat vegetables.

Makes 4 to 6 servings.

BRAISED SWEET-AND-SOUR RED CABBAGE

This is a good side dish for grilled or baked salmon, chicken breast or back bacon.

1 tbsp	olive oil
1	onion, sliced
1	large apple, cored and chopped
6 cups	shredded red cabbage
1 cup	apple cider (hard or non-alcoholic) or apple juice
3 tbsp	balsamic vinegar
1 tbsp	Splenda
1 tsp	salt
1/2 tsp	freshly ground pepper

1. In deep non-stick frying pan, heat oil over medium-high heat. Cook onion and apple for 5 minutes or until softened. Stir in cabbage and toss well. Stir in apple cider, vinegar, Splenda, salt and pepper. Reduce heat and simmer, covered, for 30 minutes or until liquid evaporates and cabbage is tender.

Makes 4 to 6 servings.

Make Ahead: Refrigerate up to 1 day and reheat over moderate heat, stirring occasionally.

RED LENTIL DAL

This is comfort food, Indian style. Serve it on its own with rice or as a side dish for simple grilled meats.

3 cups	water
1 cup	dried red lentils, rinsed and drained
1 tsp	canola oil
2	cloves garlic, minced
1	onion, chopped
1	hot chili pepper, seeded and chopped
1 tsp	minced fresh ginger
1 tsp	ground cumin
1 tsp	ground coriander
1/2 tsp	turmeric
1/4 tsp	salt
	Fresh cilantro leaves

1. In medium saucepan, combine water and lentils. Bring to boil; reduce heat, cover and simmer for 15 minutes or until lentils are tender.
2. Heat oil in non-stick frying pan over medium-high heat. Cook garlic and onion for 10 minutes or until softened and turning golden brown. Add chili pepper, ginger, cumin, coriander, turmeric and salt; cook for 2 minutes. Stir in lentils and cook for 5 minutes or until thickened and liquid is evaporated. Garnish with cilantro before serving.

Makes 4 servings.

SWEET POTATO FRIES

These fries are crispy, sweet and a little spicy—yummy!

2	sweet potatoes
2 tsp	olive oil
1/4 tsp	chili powder
1/4 tsp	paprika
Pinch	each salt and freshly ground pepper

1. Preheat oven to 425°F.
2. Peel sweet potatoes and cut into 1/2-inch sticks. Toss with oil, chili powder, paprika, salt and pepper. Place in single layer on baking sheet and bake for 20 minutes, turning once, or until tender.

Makes 4 servings.

Breakfasts and Brunches

G.I. GRANOLA

There are so many uses for this granola beyond serving it for breakfast with skim milk or low-fat yogurt: sprinkle it on fruit salad or low-fat, no-sugar ice cream, or eat a couple of handfuls as a snack.

2 cups	large-flake oats
1 cup	dried apple rings, chopped (or 1/2 cup dried cranberries or raisins)
1/2 cup	sunflower seeds
1/2 cup	sesame seeds
1/2 cup	almonds, chopped
1/2 cup	ground flaxseed
1 tbsp	cinnamon
2 tsp	grated orange zest
1/2 tsp	salt
1	egg white
1 tbsp	canola oil
1 tbsp	honey
2 tsp	frozen orange juice concentrate
1 tsp	vanilla

1. Preheat oven to 350°F.
2. In large bowl, mix together oats, apple, sunflower seeds, sesame seeds, almonds, flaxseed, cinnamon, orange zest and salt.
3. In small bowl, whisk together egg white, oil, honey, orange juice concentrate and vanilla. Pour into oat mixture and toss until thoroughly coated. Turn out onto parchment paper–lined rimmed baking sheet and spread evenly. Bake, turning mixture once with spatula halfway through, for 25 to 30 minutes or until mixture is golden brown.

Makes about 6 cups.

Make Ahead: Store in airtight container at room temperature up to 2 days or freeze up to 1 month.

HOT OATMEAL WITH PEARS AND DRIED CRANBERRIES

A satisfying hot breakfast for when there's a chill in the air. You can substitute apples, peaches or nectarines for the pears, and instead of dried cranberries, try using other dried fruits or a mixture of a few different kinds.

1 cup	steel-cut oats
2 cups	skim milk
2 cups	water
2	pears (Bosc or Bartlett), cored and chopped
1/2 cup	dried cranberries
1 tsp	cinnamon
1/4 tsp	nutmeg
	Splenda (optional)

1. Preheat oven to 300°F.
2. Place oats on rimmed baking sheet and toast in oven for 20 minutes. In large saucepan, combine milk and water and bring to boil. Stir in oats, pears, cranberries, cinnamon and nutmeg and return to boil. Reduce heat to low and cook, stirring occasionally, for 20 minutes or until thickened and oats are tender. Stir in Splenda to taste, if desired.

Makes 4 servings.

Make Ahead: Oats can be toasted and stored in airtight container at room temperature up to 1 week. Refrigerate finished oatmeal up to 1 day. Reheat, adding a little more milk or water to thin to desired consistency.

HOT KASHA CEREAL

This is a good basic hot cereal that provides a change from traditional oatmeal. Stir in some fruit or a few chopped nuts.

3 cups	water
1 cup	kasha
2 tbsp	ground flaxseed
2 tbsp	sesame seeds
2 tbsp	wheat germ
Pinch	salt
	Splenda
	cinnamon

1. In medium saucepan, bring water to boil. Add kasha, flaxseed, sesame seeds, wheat germ and salt; reduce heat to low and cook for 12 to 15 minutes, stirring occasionally.
2. Stir in Splenda and cinnamon to taste. Thin with a little water or skim milk if necessary.

Makes 4 servings.

Make Ahead: Refrigerate up to 1 day. Reheat, adding a little water or milk to thin to desired consistency.

BREAKFAST IN A GLASS

This is a great make-and-take breakfast for mornings on the run. It packs protein, fruit and fibre in one glass. Look for whey or soy protein isolate in your local health food store.

1/4 cup	flaxseed
2 tbsp	sunflower seeds
2 cups	soy milk
2 cups	fresh or frozen berries
1/2	banana
1/2 cup	low-fat yogurt
1/2 cup	whey or soy protein isolate powder
2 tbsp	soy lecithin granules (optional)

1. In spice or coffee grinder, finely grind flaxseed and sunflower seeds. Set aside.
2. In blender or food processor, blend together soy milk, berries, banana and yogurt until almost smooth.
3. Add seed mixture, protein powder and lecithin, if using, to soy milk mixture. Blend just until mixed, about 5 seconds.

Makes 2 servings.

BERRY BREAKFAST BARS

Moist and chewy, these bars are a good alternative to fat- and sugar-laden commercial cereal bars. For an extra protein kick, stir in 1/4 cup whey or soy-protein powder with the dry ingredients.

3 cups	raspberries or blueberries, or mixture of both (fresh or frozen)
1 cup	large-flake oats
1 cup	high-fibre, high-protein cereal, such as Kashi Go-Lean
1/2 cup	ground flaxseed
1/4 cup	wheat germ
1/4 cup	whole wheat flour
1/4 cup	sesame seeds
2 tsp	cinnamon
2	egg whites
1/4 cup	frozen apple juice concentrate
2 tsp	vanilla

1. Preheat oven to 350°F.
2. In large bowl, stir together berries, oats, cereal, flaxseed, wheat germ, flour, sesame seeds and cinnamon.
3. In small bowl, whisk together egg whites, apple juice concentrate and vanilla. Add to dry mixture, stirring to thoroughly moisten.
4. Press into oiled 8-inch square baking pan. Bake for 35 to 40 minutes or until lightly golden and firm. Let cool. Cut into bars.

Makes 16.

Make Ahead: Refrigerate in airtight container up to 5 days or freeze up to 1 month.

OATMEAL BUTTERMILK PANCAKES

Make pancake breakfasts a weekend tradition. Serve them with fresh fruit or applesauce.

3/4 cup	large-flake oats
2 cups	buttermilk
1 cup	whole wheat flour
1/4 cup	ground flaxseed
1 tbsp	Splenda
1 tsp	cinnamon
1 tsp	baking soda
1 tsp	baking powder
1/4 tsp	salt
1/2 cup	liquid egg
2 tbsp	canola oil
1 tsp	vanilla

1. In bowl, soak oats in buttermilk for 20 minutes.
2. In large bowl, combine flour, flaxseed, Splenda, cinnamon, baking soda, baking powder and salt.
3. In another bowl, whisk together egg, oil and vanilla. Stir in soaked oats and buttermilk. Pour over flour mixture and stir until just mixed.
4. Meanwhile, heat non-stick griddle or large non-stick frying pan over medium heat. Ladle about 1/4 cup batter onto griddle for each pancake. Cook until bubbles appear on top, about 2 minutes.
5. Using spatula, flip pancakes and cook for another 2 minutes or until golden. Transfer to plate and cover to keep warm. Repeat with remaining batter.

Makes 16 pancakes, 4 to 6 servings.

COTTAGE CHEESE PANCAKES

These pancakes are light and fluffy, full of little pockets of melted cottage cheese. Serve them with fresh fruit, berries or applesauce.

1 1/2 cups	low-fat cottage cheese
1/2 cup	buttermilk
2	egg whites
1	omega-3 egg
1 tbsp	canola oil
1 tsp	vanilla
1 tsp	grated lemon zest
1/2 cup	whole wheat flour
1/2 cup	wheat germ
1 tbsp	Splenda
1/2 tsp	baking soda
1/4 tsp	baking powder

1. In large bowl, combine cottage cheese, buttermilk, egg whites, egg, oil, vanilla and lemon zest. In another bowl, stir together flour, wheat germ, Splenda, baking soda and baking powder. Add flour mixture to cottage cheese mixture and stir until combined.
2. Heat non-stick griddle or large non-stick frying pan over medium heat. Ladle about 1/4 cup batter onto griddle for each pancake. Cook for about 2 minutes or until bubbles appear on top. Using spatula, carefully flip pancake and cook for another 2 minutes or until underside is golden. Transfer to plate and cover to keep warm. Repeat with remaining batter.

Makes 4 servings.

CRUNCHY BAKED FRENCH TOAST

This crispy, nutty coating takes simple French toast to another level. Serve with fruit, or with the berry filling from Berry-Stuffed French Toast (see recipe, page 216) and Sweetened Yogurt Cheese (see recipe, page 248).

1/3 cup	ground almonds
1/3 cup	ground flaxseed
1/3 cup	oats
2 tbsp	Splenda
1 tsp	cinnamon
3	omega-3 eggs
2	egg whites
1 cup	skim milk
1 tsp	vanilla
6	slices whole-grain bread

1. Preheat oven to 400°F.
2. In shallow dish or pie plate, mix together almonds, flaxseed, oats, Splenda and cinnamon.
3. In medium bowl, whisk together eggs, egg whites, skim milk and vanilla.
4. Dip bread slices into egg mixture, turning to coat well. Let each slice soak in mixture for 2 minutes. Remove bread slice from milk mixture and place on nut mixture, pressing to adhere. Turn slice over and press to coat other side. Repeat with remaining bread slices and place on lightly oiled baking sheet.
5. Bake for 10 minutes; turn and bake for another 10 minutes or until coating is crisp.

Makes 6 servings.

BERRY-STUFFED FRENCH TOAST

This is a perfect dish for brunch entertaining. Keep the finished toast warm on a baking sheet in a 150°F oven until ready to serve.

Berry Filling:

4 cups	mixed field berries (fresh or frozen)
3 tbsp	Splenda
1 tsp	grated lemon zest
1 tbsp	cornstarch

French Toast:

2 cups	skim milk
1¼ cups	liquid egg
1 tbsp	Splenda
2 tsp	vanilla
1 tsp	cinnamon
2 tbsp	canola oil (approx.)
12	slices whole-grain bread

1. **Berry Filling:** In saucepan over medium heat, combine berries, Splenda and lemon zest; cook for about 5 minutes or until Splenda is dissolved and berries have released some of their juice. In small bowl, blend cornstarch with 1 tbsp juice from berries; stir into berry mixture. Increase heat to high and cook, stirring constantly, for about 5 minutes or until thickened. Remove from heat and set aside.
2. **French Toast:** In large bowl, whisk together milk, egg, Splenda, vanilla and cinnamon.
3. Brush 1 tsp oil onto large non-stick frying pan over medium-high heat. Dip bread, 1 slice at a time, into egg mixture, pressing down and letting soak for 10 seconds, then pressing and soaking the other side. Lift out, letting excess mixture drip back into bowl. Fry soaked bread slices, 2 at a time (4 at a time if using griddle), for 3 minutes; turn 1 piece over and evenly spread golden brown side with 2 heaping tbsp of the berry filling. Flip second slice, cooked side down, onto filling to form sandwich; press firmly with back of spatula. Continue frying for 3 minutes; turn sandwich over and fry for 3 minutes longer or until golden brown on both sides. Repeat with remaining bread slices, brushing griddle with more oil as needed.

4. Put any leftover berry filling in bowl and serve alongside toasts.

Makes 6 servings.

Make Ahead: Refrigerate berry mixture up to 3 days.

TOFU BREAKFAST BURRITO

The tofu filling in these burritos is a tasty alternative to scrambled eggs and can also be served with a slice of high-fibre toast.

1 tbsp	olive oil
1	small onion, chopped
1	clove garlic, minced
1/2 cup	chopped red pepper
1 lb	firm tofu, crumbled
1/2 tsp	turmeric
2	drops hot pepper sauce, or to taste
Pinch	each salt and pepper
6	small whole wheat tortillas
1/2 cup	light-style cheddar cheese
	Low-fat salsa

1. In non-stick frying pan, heat oil over medium-high heat. Cook onion, garlic and red pepper for 8 minutes or until softened. Add tofu, turmeric, hot pepper sauce, salt and pepper; stir to combine. Cook for 5 minutes or until heated through and any liquid is evaporated.
2. Divide mixture among tortillas. Sprinkle with cheese and roll up. Serve with salsa.

Makes 6 servings.

BACON AND EGG MUFFINS

Two of these muffins make a delicious portable breakfast.

1 tsp	olive oil
1	onion, chopped
1	small jalapeño pepper, finely chopped (optional)
4	slices peameal bacon or ham, chopped
1	can (14 oz) artichoke hearts, drained and chopped
3/4 cup	wheat bran
1/2 cup	shredded light-style Swiss cheese
1/4 cup	chopped fresh basil or parsley
1 1/2 cups	liquid egg
3/4 cup	skim milk
1 tsp	freshly ground pepper

1. Preheat oven to 350°F. Line 12 muffin tins with paper or foil liners.
2. In non-stick frying pan, heat oil over medium-high heat. Cook onion and jalapeño, if using, for 5 minutes or until softened. Transfer to bowl and allow to cool for 5 minutes. Stir in bacon, artichokes, wheat bran, cheese and basil.
3. In separate bowl, whisk together egg, milk and pepper. Pour into bacon and onion mixture and stir until well combined.
4. Carefully ladle into muffin tins, filling to top.
5. Bake for 25 minutes or until filling is firm and tops are slightly brown. Let cool on rack for 5 minutes. Carefully remove muffins from tin and allow to cool completely.

Makes 12 muffins.

Make Ahead: Wrap muffins individually in plastic wrap and refrigerate up to 2 days or freeze up to 1 month. Reheat in microwave for 30 seconds on high.

HAM AND CHEESE BREAKFAST MUFFINS

Make these on a weekend and you are set for the week. Great for a grab-and-go morning.

1½ cups	whole wheat flour
1 cup	wheat bran
2 tsp	baking powder
1 tsp	baking soda
½ tsp	cayenne pepper (optional)
Pinch	salt
1½ cups	low-fat yogurt
1	omega-3 egg, beaten
½ cup	skim milk
2 tbsp	olive oil
4 oz	ham, chopped
¾ cup	light-style cheddar cheese
¼ cup	chopped green onions

1. Preheat oven to 375°F. Line 12 muffin tins with paper or foil liners.
2. In large bowl, stir together flour, wheat bran, baking powder, baking soda, cayenne, if using, and salt.
3. In another bowl, whisk together yogurt, egg, milk and oil. Stir in ham, cheese and green onion.
4. Make well in centre of dry ingredients; add wet ingredients and stir just until moistened. Spoon into muffin tins. Bake for 20 to 25 minutes or until tester inserted in centre comes out clean.

Makes 12 muffins.

Make Ahead: Wrap well individually and refrigerate up to 3 days or freeze up to 1 month. Reheat in microwave for 30 seconds on high.

SMOKED SALMON SCRAMBLED EGGS

Smoked salmon makes scrambled eggs elegant and special. Serve with a slice of high-fibre toast.

4	egg whites
2	omega-3 eggs
2 tbsp	skim milk
1/4 tsp	freshly ground pepper
1 tsp	canola oil
2 oz	smoked salmon, chopped
1 tbsp	chopped fresh chives or dill

1. In bowl, whisk together egg whites, eggs, milk and pepper.
2. In non-stick frying pan, heat oil over medium heat. Add egg mixture. Using rubber spatula, gently stir eggs until almost set. Stir in salmon and continue to cook, stirring gently, until eggs are set but still slightly creamy. Stir in chives.

Makes 2 servings.

CHEESE BLINTZES

Purchase the solid, dry or pressed-style cottage cheese for this brunch favourite. Serve with seasonal fruits or berries or with the berry filling from Berry-Stuffed French Toast (see recipe, page 216).

1/2 cup	whole wheat flour
1 tbsp	ground flaxseed or wheat germ
Pinch	salt
2	omega-3 eggs
1 cup	skim milk
1 tsp	vanilla
1 tbsp	canola oil

Filling:

8 oz	dry solid-curd cottage cheese
1	egg
1/2 cup	non-fat plain or vanilla yogurt with sweetener
2 tbsp	Splenda
1 tsp	grated lemon zest

1. In medium bowl, combine flour, flaxseed and salt. In another bowl, whisk together eggs, milk and vanilla. Pour liquid mixture over flour mixture and whisk until smooth. Let batter stand at room temperature for at least 15 minutes or cover and refrigerate for up to 2 hours.
2. Preheat oven to 350°F. Line a baking sheet with parchment paper.
3. Brush small non-stick or crepe pan with just enough oil to lightly coat it. Heat pan over medium heat. Pour in 1/4 cup batter, swirling pan to cover the bottom. Cook crepe until firm and slightly golden, about 2 minutes. Flip crepe and cook on other side for another 30 seconds. Remove to plate. Repeat with remaining batter, stacking crepes on top of each other.
4. **Filling:** In large bowl, blend together cottage cheese, egg, yogurt, Splenda and lemon zest.
5. Place crepes flat on work surface. Divide filling among crepes, placing in centre of each. Fold in sides and place blintzes on prepared baking sheet, folded side down. Bake for 25 to 30 minutes or until heated through.

Makes 8 blintzes, 4 servings.

HERBED CHEESE OMELETTE

You can use 3 or 4 medium-size cooked shrimp instead of the chicken in this omelette, or add some chopped red pepper and/or celery to the spinach.

1/2 cup	liquid egg
2 tbsp	herbed extra low-fat soft cheese (such as Boursin)
1 tbsp	water
1 tbsp	chopped fresh basil (optional)
1 tsp	grated lemon zest
1 tsp	lemon juice
Pinch	each salt and freshly ground pepper
1 tsp	olive oil
1/2 cup	tightly packed chopped fresh spinach or Swiss chard
1	slice deli chicken breast or ham, chopped

1. In bowl, combine egg, cheese, water, basil, if using, lemon zest and juice, salt and pepper. Using fork, stir just until blended and cheese is broken up into smaller lumps.
2. In small non-stick frying pan, heat oil over medium-high heat. Add spinach; cover and cook for about 2 minutes or until spinach is wilted. Pour in egg mixture and cook, uncovered, for about 5 minutes or until almost set, lifting edges to allow uncooked eggs to run underneath.
3. Sprinkle chicken over half of the omelette. Using spatula, fold over other half and cook for 1 minute. Slide onto warmed plate.

Makes 1 serving.

BROCCOLI, SUN-DRIED TOMATO AND FETA QUICHE

Serve this easy crustless quiche warm or cold. It pairs well with a side salad for lunch or a light supper.

1 tsp	non-hydrogenated margarine
1/4 cup	fresh whole wheat breadcrumbs
1	bunch broccoli, trimmed and cut into florets
1 1/4 cups	liquid egg
1 cup	skim milk
1/4 tsp	each salt and freshly ground pepper
2 slices	fresh whole-grain bread, cubed
2	green onions, chopped
1/4 cup	packed sun-dried tomatoes, rehydrated in 1 cup hot water, drained and chopped
2 oz	light-style feta cheese, crumbled

1. Preheat oven to 350°F. Grease bottom and sides of deep 10-inch pie plate with margarine. Add bread crumbs, tilting to coat bottom and sides evenly.
2. Steam broccoli for 5 minutes or until tender-crisp. Rinse under cold water, drain and chop. Set aside.
3. In large bowl, whisk together egg, milk, salt and pepper. Stir in steamed broccoli, cubed bread, green onions, sun-dried tomatoes and feta. Pour into prepared pan.
4. Bake for 50 to 60 minutes or until light golden, puffed and just set in centre.

Makes 6 servings.

Variations:

Quiche Lorraine: Omit broccoli, sun-dried tomatoes and feta. Stir 1/4 cup shredded light-style Swiss cheese and 4 slices back bacon, chopped, into egg mixture before baking.

Caramelized Onion, Roasted Red Pepper and Chèvre: Omit broccoli, sun-dried tomatoes, feta and green onion. In non-stick frying pan, heat 2 tsp oil over medium heat. Cook 3 onions, thinly sliced, for about 30 minutes or until golden brown. Stir into egg mixture along with 1/2 cup chopped roasted red peppers and 2 oz, chèvre, crumbled, before baking.

Smoked Salmon: Omit broccoli, sun-dried tomatoes and feta. Stir 4 oz chopped smoked salmon and 2 tbsp chopped fresh dill into egg mixture before baking.

BAKED EGGS IN HAM CUPS

Dress this dish up by serving the cups on a platter of mixed greens.

6	slices lean ham (without holes)
1½ cups	liquid egg
3 tbsp	skim milk
¼ cup	chopped green onions
1 tbsp	grated Parmesan cheese
¼ tsp	each salt and freshly ground pepper

1. Preheat oven to 400°F.
2. Carefully ease 1 slice ham into each of 6 lightly oiled muffin tins (edges will be higher than edges of tins).
3. In bowl, whisk together egg and milk. Stir in green onions, Parmesan, salt and pepper.
4. Divide egg mixture evenly among ham cups. Bake for 15 minutes or until knife inserted in centre comes out clean. Use 2 spoons to carefully remove from pan.

Makes 6 servings.

SAUSAGE AND SPINACH EGG ROULADE

This rolled omelette is beautiful to serve for a weekend brunch.

2 tsp	olive oil
8 oz	chicken or turkey sausage, casing removed and crumbled
2	cloves garlic, minced
1	pkg (10 oz) frozen chopped spinach, thawed and squeezed dry
1/4 cup	cream cheese
1/4 tsp	each salt and freshly ground pepper
4	egg whites
3	omega-3 eggs
1/4 cup	skim milk
2 tbsp	grated Parmesan cheese

1. Preheat oven to 375°F. Grease 13- x 9-inch baking pan and line bottom with parchment paper.
2. In non-stick frying pan, heat oil over medium-high heat. Cook sausage and garlic until sausage is cooked through, about 5 minutes. Stir in spinach, cream cheese, salt and pepper until well combined. Cover and set aside.
3. In bowl, whisk together egg whites, eggs, milk and Parmesan; pour into prepared pan. Bake for 10 to 12 minutes or until firm. Invert onto work surface; peel off paper. Spread sausage mixture evenly over top. Starting at narrow end, roll up, jelly roll style. Slice in rounds to serve.

Makes 4 servings.

MACARONI FRITTATA

This frittata is an ingenious way to use up leftover pasta.

2 tsp	olive oil
1	onion, chopped
1	clove garlic, minced
1	zucchini, thinly sliced
4 oz	mushrooms, sliced
1 1/2 cups	liquid egg
1 1/2 cups	cooked whole wheat macaroni
1/2 cup	frozen peas
1/4 cup	skim milk
Pinch	each salt and freshly ground pepper
1/2 cup	shredded light-style Swiss cheese

1. In large non-stick frying pan with ovenproof handle, heat oil over medium-high heat; add onion, garlic, zucchini and mushrooms. Cook, stirring, for about 5 minutes or until softened.

2. Meanwhile, in bowl, whisk together egg, macaroni, peas, milk, salt and pepper. Pour into frying pan, stirring to combine. Sprinkle with cheese and cook for about 10 minutes or until almost firm but top is still slightly runny. Place under broiler for about 3 minutes or until frittata is golden brown. Slice into wedges.

Makes 4 servings.

Muffins and Breads

CARROT MUFFINS

These healthful muffins are a delightful source of fibre.

1 cup	whole wheat flour
1/2 cup	wheat bran
1/2 cup	ground flaxseed
1/4 cup	Splenda
2 tsp	baking powder
1/2 tsp	baking soda
2 tsp	cinnamon
1 tsp	ground ginger
1/4 tsp	salt
1 cup	buttermilk
1/2 cup	liquid egg
1/4 cup	canola oil
1 tsp	vanilla
1 1/2 cup	finely grated carrot
1/2 cup	raisins, softened in hot water for 10 minutes and drained
1/3 cup	chopped pecans

1. Preheat oven to 375°F. Line 12 muffin tins with paper or foil liners.
2. In large bowl, combine flour, wheat bran, flaxseed, Splenda, baking powder, baking soda, cinnamon, ginger and salt. In small bowl, whisk together buttermilk, egg, oil and vanilla. Stir in carrot, raisins and pecans. Add flour mixture and stir just until combined.
3. Divide batter among muffin tins. Bake for 20 to 25 minutes or until tester inserted in centre of muffin comes out clean.

Makes 12 muffins.

Make Ahead: Store at room temperature up to 2 days or wrap and freeze in resealable plastic bag or airtight container up to 1 month.

MIXED BERRY MUFFINS

Not your average bran muffin. These are moist and packed with berries.

1 cup	All-Bran or 100% Bran cereal
1 cup	wheat bran
1 1/2 cups	buttermilk
1/2 cup	liquid egg
1/4 cup	canola oil
1 tsp	vanilla
1 cup	whole wheat flour
1/2 cup	Splenda
1 tsp	baking soda
1/2 tsp	baking powder
1 1/2 cups	mixture of blueberries and raspberries (fresh or frozen)

1. Preheat oven to 350°F. Line 12 muffin tins with paper or foil liners.
2. In large bowl, combine cereal and wheat bran. Stir in buttermilk; set aside for 5 minutes. Stir in egg, oil and vanilla.
3. In separate large bowl, combine flour, Splenda, baking soda and baking powder. Stir into cereal mixture just until moistened. Stir in berries.
4. Divide batter among muffin tins. Bake for about 25 minutes or until tester inserted in centre comes out clean.

Makes 12 muffins.

Make Ahead: Store at room temperature up to 2 days or wrap and freeze in resealable plastic bag or airtight container up to 1 month.

ORANGE-CRANBERRY BRAN MUFFINS

The cranberries give these moist muffins a nice little burst of tartness. Have one for a mid-morning snack.

1/2 cup	wheat bran
1/2 cup	All-Bran or 100% Bran cereal
1/2 cup	boiling water
1 cup	buttermilk
1	omega-3 egg
1/3 cup	Splenda
1/4 cup	canola oil
1 tbsp	frozen orange juice concentrate
1 tsp	grated orange zest
1 tsp	vanilla
1 cup	whole wheat flour
3/4 cup	ground flaxseed
1 1/2 tsp	baking soda
1 tsp	cinnamon
1/2 tsp	ground ginger
1/4 tsp	salt
1 1/2 cups	fresh or frozen cranberries, roughly chopped
1/4 cup	toasted pumpkin seeds (optional) (see page 233)

1. Preheat oven to 400°F. Line 12 muffin tins with paper or foil liners.
2. In large bowl, combine wheat bran and cereal. Stir in boiling water to moisten; let cool for 5 minutes. Stir in buttermilk, egg, Splenda, oil, orange juice, orange zest and vanilla.
3. In separate large bowl, combine flour, flaxseed, baking soda, cinnamon, ginger and salt; mix in cranberries, and pumpkin seeds, if using. Add to bran mixture, stirring until just combined.
4. Divide batter among muffin tins. Bake for about 25 minutes or until tester inserted in centre comes out clean.

Makes 12 muffins.

Make Ahead: Store at room temperature up to 2 days or wrap and freeze in resealable plastic bag or airtight container up to 1 month.

Toasting pumpkin seeds: Place seeds in dry frying pan over medium heat. Toast, stirring occasionally, for 5 minutes or until popping and fragrant.

CHOCOLATE ZUCCHINI MUFFINS

An unlikely but delicious combination.

1 cup	whole wheat flour
1/2 cup	oat bran
1/2 cup	cocoa powder
1/4 cup	wheat germ
2 tsp	baking powder
1 tsp	baking soda
1/4 tsp	salt
3/4 cup	brown sugar substitute
1 cup	skim milk
1/2 cup	liquid egg
1/4 cup	canola oil
1 tbsp	vanilla
2 cups	grated zucchini

1. Preheat oven to 400°F. Line 12 muffin tins with paper or foil liners.
2. In large bowl, combine flour, oat bran, cocoa, wheat germ, baking powder, baking soda and salt.
3. In another bowl, whisk together brown sugar substitute, milk, egg, oil and vanilla. Stir into flour mixture. Add zucchini and stir until ingredients are just moistened. Divide batter among muffin tins. Bake for 20 minutes or until cake tester inserted in centre comes out clean.

Makes 12 muffins.

Make Ahead: Store at room temperature up to 2 days or wrap and freeze in resealable plastic bag or airtight container up to 1 month.

BLUEBERRY ROCK CAKES

You can substitute any berry in this; just adjust the amount of Splenda accordingly.

1	omega-3 egg
1/2 cup	Splenda
1/2 cup	skim milk
1/4 cup	canola oil
1 1/4 cups	whole wheat flour
1/2 cup	rolled oats
1/4 cup	wheat bran
2 tbsp	poppy seeds
1 tbsp	baking powder
1/2 tsp	grated lemon zest
1/2 tsp	cinnamon
1/2 tsp	salt
3/4 cup	fresh or frozen wild blueberries

1. Preheat oven to 375°F. Line a baking sheet with parchment paper.
2. In large bowl, whisk together egg, Splenda, milk and oil.
3. In another bowl, mix together flour, oats, wheat bran, poppy seeds, baking powder, lemon zest, cinnamon and salt. Stir egg mixture into flour mixture just until combined. Gently stir in blueberries.
4. Drop batter in 8 mounds onto prepared baking sheet. Bake until firm and golden brown, 15 to 20 minutes. Remove to rack and let cool.

Makes 8 rock cakes.

Make Ahead: Best eaten the day they are made, but can be frozen in resealable plastic bag up to 1 month.

SMOKED SALMON AND DILL SCONES

These scones are ideal snacks because they contain a good mix of protein and fibre. They also make a nice addition at brunch.

1 cup	whole wheat flour
1 cup	wheat bran
1/2 tsp	baking soda
1/4 tsp	each salt and freshly ground pepper
5 oz	smoked salmon, chopped
1/4 cup	chopped fresh dill
1/2 cup	non-fat sour cream
1 cup	buttermilk (approx.)
1	omega-3 egg, lightly beaten
	Dill Cream (see below), optional

1. Preheat oven to 425°F.
2. In large bowl, combine flour, bran, baking soda, salt and pepper. Stir in salmon and dill. Add sour cream and just enough buttermilk to make a soft, sticky dough.
3. Turn out dough onto floured surface; knead gently 6 times or until smooth. Pat out to 3/4-inch thickness. Cut dough into 2-inch rounds. Place on baking sheet and brush tops with beaten egg. Bake for about 15 minutes or until golden on bottom. Serve with Dill Cream, if desired.

Makes 12 scones.

DILL CREAM

This also makes a great dip for veggies.

1/2 cup	low-fat sour cream or Yogurt Cheese (see recipe, page 248)
1/4 cup	chopped fresh dill
1 tsp	lemon juice
1	clove garlic, minced

1. In bowl, stir together all ingredients.

Maks about 3/4 cup.

CRAN-APPLE OATMEAL BARS

Tuck these nutritious treats into packed lunches.

3 cups	large-flake oats
1 1/2 cups	whole wheat flour
2 tsp	cinnamon
1 tsp	baking powder
1 tsp	baking soda
1/4 tsp	salt
3/4 cup	Splenda
1/4 cup	non-hydrogenated margarine
1	omega-3 egg
1	egg white
3/4 cup	unsweetened applesauce
2 tsp	vanilla
1 cup	dried cranberries

1. Preheat oven to 350°F. Lin a 13- x 9-inch baking pan with parchment paper.
2. In large bowl, combine oats, whole wheat flour, cinnamon, baking powder, baking soda and salt.
3. In another bowl, beat together Splenda and margarine until fluffy. Beat in egg, egg white, applesauce and vanilla. Add oat mixture and stir to combine. Stir in cranberries. Scrape dough into prepared baking pan and bake for 20 minutes or until cake tester inserted in centre comes out clean. Let cool completely and cut into bars.

Makes 24 bars.

BANANA BREAD

Spread a slice of this quick bread with a teaspoon of light cream cheese.

1 1/2 cups	whole wheat flour
3/4 cup	ground flaxseed
2 tsp	baking powder
1 tsp	baking soda
1 tsp	cinnamon
1/2 tsp	salt
1 cup	mashed very ripe banana (about 3)
3/4 cup	Splenda
3/4 cup	buttermilk
1/2 cup	liquid egg
1 tsp	vanilla

1. Preheat oven to 350°F. Oil a 9- by 5-inch loaf pan.
2. In bowl, stir together flour, flaxseed, baking powder, baking soda, cinnamon and salt.
3. In another bowl, mix together banana, Splenda, buttermilk, egg and vanilla. Pour into flour mixture and stir just until moistened.
4. Pour batter into prepared pan. Bake for 45 to 50 minutes or until tester inserted in centre comes out clean. Let cool on rack.

Makes 1 loaf.

Make Ahead: Wrap in plastic wrap or foil and store at room temperature up to 3 days or freeze up to 1 month.

STRAWBERRY TEA BREAD

This recipe makes two loaves, one for now and one for the freezer. A slice makes a perfect snack or delicious dessert paired with sliced berries.

1 1/2 cups	whole wheat flour
1 1/2 cups	rolled oats
1/2 cup	wheat bran
1 tsp	cinnamon
1 tsp	baking soda
1/2 tsp	baking powder
1/2 tsp	salt
3/4 cup	liquid egg
3/4 cup	Splenda
1/2 cup	canola oil
1/2 cup	skim milk
1 tsp	vanilla
4 cups	strawberries, fresh or frozen and thawed, mashed

1. Preheat oven to 375°F. Oil 2 9- x 5-inch loaf pans.
2. In large bowl, stir together flour, oats, bran, cinnamon, baking soda, baking powder and salt; set aside.
3. In separate bowl, whisk together egg, Splenda, oil, milk and vanilla. Pour over dry ingredients and stir just until moistened. Stir in strawberries.
4. Divide mixture evenly between prepared pans.
5. Bake for 45 to 50 minutes or until cake tester inserted in centre comes out clean. Let cool in pan on rack for 15 minutes. Turn out onto rack and let cool completely.

Makes 2 loaves.

Make Ahead: Wrap in plastic wrap or foil and store at room temperature up to 3 days, or wrap in plastic wrap and heavy-duty foil and freeze up to 1 month.

WHOLE WHEAT SODA BREAD

This is such an easy way to make delicious bread. Use it to make open-faced sandwiches or spread a slice with a little sugar-free jam for a snack.

3 cups	whole wheat flour
1/2 cup	wheat bran
1 tsp	baking soda
1/2 tsp	baking powder
1/2 tsp	salt
1 1/2 cups	buttermilk
1	omega-3 egg

1. Preheat oven to 425°F.
2. In large bowl, stir together flour, bran, baking soda, baking powder and salt.
3. In another bowl, whisk together buttermilk and egg. Add to flour mixture, stirring gently until mixture forms a soft, sticky dough.
4. Turn out onto lightly floured surface. Knead dough gently into ball. Place on floured baking sheet. With sharp knife, cut large X in top of loaf. Bake for 40 minutes or until golden and tester inserted in centre comes out clean.

Makes 1 loaf.

Variation: Mix in 2 tbsp sunflower seeds or sesame seeds, or 1/3 cup chopped dried apricots, along with the flour.

BREAD MACHINE GRANARY LOAF

There's nothing like home-baked bread, and this one, submitted by reader Elaine, is easily made in a bread machine.

1	omega-3 egg, lightly beaten
1 cup	water
1 tbsp	honey
1 tbsp	olive oil
2 cups	whole wheat flour
1/2 cup	wheat bran
1/4 cup	pumpkin seeds
1/4 cup	sunflower seeds
1 tsp	salt
1 1/2 tsp	active dry yeast or bread machine yeast

1. Add egg, water, honey and oil to bread machine canister.
2. In bowl, stir together flour, bran, pumpkin seeds, sunflower seeds and salt. Pour over liquid ingredients; do not stir. Sprinkle yeast on top.
3. Bake according to manufacturer's instructions.

Makes 1 loaf (1 1/2 lb).

Desserts

TEA-INFUSED FRUIT SALAD

You can use any type of fruit in this salad—just make sure it's mostly green-light. For an elegant presentation, serve in glass dessert dishes or large wineglasses. If you'd like, you can sprinkle the fruit with some sunflower or pumpkin seeds and serve with a dollop of yogurt or low-fat, no-sugar ice cream.

1 cup	hot brewed herbal mixed fruit or berry tea
1 tbsp	frozen orange juice concentrate
1 tsp	Splenda or honey
1 tsp	vanilla
1 tsp	cardamom
2 cups	hulled strawberries, halved
2	kiwis, peeled and sliced
2	ripe pears, cored and cut into bite-size chunks
1	each orange and grapefruit, peeled and sectioned
1	large apple, cored and cut into bite-size chunks
1	banana, peeled and sliced
1 cup	blueberries, blackberries or raspberries
	Seeds of 1/2 pomegranate

1. In small bowl, whisk together hot tea, orange juice concentrate, Splenda, vanilla and cardamom. Let cool to room temperature.
2. In large bowl, combine strawberries, kiwis, pears, orange, grapefruit, apple, banana, blueberries, and pomegranate seeds.
3. Pour tea mixture over fruit and gently stir to mix well.

Makes 6 to 8 servings.

Make Ahead: Cover and refrigerate up to 1 day.

GRILLED FRUIT KABOBS WITH LEMON-YOGURT SAUCE

Here's a simple way to turn plain fruit into something special. You can add a small amount of yellow-light pineapple.

4 cups	green-light fruit

Choose from mixture of:

- Cubed pitted peaches, nectarines or plums
- Seedless orange segments
- Seedless grapes
- Pitted sweet cherries

Lemon-Yogurt Sauce:

1 cup	low-fat plain yogurt
1/4 cup	Splenda
2 tbsp	lemon juice
2 tsp	chopped fresh lemon balm or mint
2 tsp	grated lemon zest
	Lemon balm or mint sprigs for garnish

1. Preheat oiled grill to medium-high.
2. Thread fruit alternately onto each of 8 metal or soaked wooden skewers. Grill for 4 minutes per side or until fruit is warm and lightly browned.
3. **Yogurt Sauce:** In bowl, stir together yogurt, Splenda, lemon juice, chopped lemon balm and lemon zest.
4. Drizzle some of the yogurt sauce over kabobs. Garnish plates with sprig of lemon balm. Pour rest of sauce into bowl for dipping.

Makes 4 servings.

ROSEWATER-CITRUS COMPOTE

You can use any mixture of citrus in this wonderfully fragrant dessert. Try oranges, tangerines, clementines and blood oranges.

3 tbsp	rosewater*
2 tbsp	Splenda
4 cups	peeled and segmented citrus fruit (such as oranges, tangerines and clementines)
1/4 tsp	ground cardamom
1/2 cup	low-fat vanilla yogurt with sweetener
3 tbsp	chopped pistachios

1. Heat rosewater and Splenda in saucepan over medium heat until just warm. Stir in citrus fruit and cardamom, tossing to coat well with rosewater mixture. Transfer to bowl and allow to stand at room temperature for at least 1 hour before serving, stirring occasionally.
2. To serve, spoon fruit into serving bowls and top with a dollop of yogurt and sprinkle of pistachios.

Makes 4 to 6 servings.

* Rosewater is available at some supermarkets and at Middle Eastern grocery stores.

LEMON SOUR CREAM ICE CREAM

The non-fat sour cream in this ice cream gives it such a creamy texture, you'll swear you're cheating.

2 cups	non-fat sour cream
1 cup	non-fat plain yogurt
1/2 cup	Splenda
	Zest and juice of 1 lemon

1. In bowl, whisk together sour cream, yogurt, Splenda, lemon zest and juice until Splenda is dissolved. Pour into ice cream maker and freeze according to manufacturer's instructions. Alternatively, pour mixture into an 8- or 9-inch metal cake pan and freeze until firm, about 2 hours. Cut into chunks and, working in batches, place frozen chunks in food processor. Purée until smooth, scrape into airtight container and freeze until firm.
2. Before serving, soften ice cream in refrigerator for 15 minutes.

Makes 4 cups, 6 to 8 servings.

STRAWBERRIES AND CREAM PHYLLO CUPS

This is an elegant yet simple dessert.

2	sheets phyllo pastry
2 tsp	olive oil
2 cups	sliced strawberries
1 tbsp	Splenda
1 tbsp	balsamic vinegar
1½ cups	Sweetened Yogurt Cheese (see below)
	Fresh mint sprigs

1. Preheat oven to 400°F.
2. Lay sheet of phyllo on work surface. Brush with 1 tsp oil. Using knife, cut into three 5-inch wide strips; fold each strip into thirds to form a square. Gently mould into muffin tins. Repeat with remaining phyllo and oil to make 6 shells. Bake for 5 minutes or until golden.
3. In bowl, toss together strawberries, Splenda and vinegar. Allow to sit for about 15 minutes.
4. Divide Sweetened Yogurt Cheese among phyllo cups. Top with strawberry mixture and garnish with mint.

Makes 6 servings.

Make Ahead: Phyllo cups can be stored in an airtight container up to 1 week.

Yogurt Cheese: Place plain non- or low-fat yogurt in sieve lined with cheesecloth or a coffee filter. Place sieve over a bowl. Cover with plastic wrap and refrigerate at least 1 hour or up to 4 hours. Discard liquid that drains off and transfer yogurt to another bowl.

Sweetened Yogurt Cheese: Make Yogurt Cheese as instructed above. Add Splenda to taste.

CHOCOLATE PUDDING

Ruth loves chocolate and strawberries. This dessert is one of her favourites.

1/4 cup	cocoa powder
1/4 cup	cornstarch (or 2 tbsp arrowroot)
2 tbsp	Splenda
1/4 tsp	salt
2 cups	skim milk
2 tsp	vanilla
1 cup	raspberries or sliced strawberries, or mixture (optional)

1. In saucepan, stir together cocoa, cornstarch, Splenda and salt. Add milk and vanilla and cook over medium-high heat, stirring constantly, until boiling and thickened. Continue cooking, stirring, for 3 minutes. Remove from heat and stir in berries, if using.

2. Pour into serving bowl or 4 individual serving dishes. Let cool to room temperature or place plastic wrap directly on surface and chill in refrigerator before serving.

Makes 4 servings.

Make Ahead: Refrigerate up to 2 days.

CREAMY RASPBERRY MOUSSE

No one will know this dessert is so easy to make. Serve as is or dress it up with some fresh fruit or berries.

2 cups	low-fat cottage cheese
2 cups	frozen raspberries
1/4 cup	Splenda
1 tbsp	amaretto or berry-flavoured liqueur (optional)

1. In blender or food processor, process cottage cheese, raspberries, Splenda and amaretto, if using.

Makes 4 servings.

Make Ahead: Refrigerate in airtight container up to 3 days.

APPLE PUDDING

Cool, creamy and refreshing.

1/4 cup	apple juice
1 tbsp	gelatin
1 cup	silken tofu, drained
2 tbsp	Splenda
1 tsp	vanilla
1/2 tsp	cinnamon
1 cup	unsweetened applesauce

1. Pour apple juice into small saucepan and sprinkle gelatin over top; let stand for 1 minute. Place over medium heat and stir until gelatin dissolves.
2. In bowl, whisk together tofu, Splenda, vanilla and cinnamon. Add applesauce and gelatin mixture and stir until thoroughly combined. Divide evenly among 4 glass dishes. Refrigerate for about 2 hours or until firm.

Makes 4 servings.

Make Ahead: Refrigerate up to 3 days.

FRUITY QUINOA PUDDING

This firm pudding can also be served for breakfast.

2 1/2 cups	water
1 1/4 cups	quinoa, rinsed and drained
2 cups	skim milk
2 cups	berries (fresh or frozen)
3/4 cup	chopped dried apples
1/2 cup	liquid egg
1/4 cup	frozen apple juice concentrate
1/4 cup	Splenda
1 tsp	cinnamon
1/2 tsp	ground ginger
1/4 tsp	ground nutmeg
Pinch	salt
1/2 cup	chopped hazelnuts or almonds

1. Preheat oven to 350°F.
2. In medium saucepan, bring water to boil. Add quinoa, reduce heat and simmer, covered, for 15 minutes or until liquid is absorbed.
3. In large bowl, stir together cooked quinoa, milk, berries, apples, egg, apple juice concentrate, Splenda, cinnamon, ginger, nutmeg and salt. Pour into oiled 8-inch square baking dish; sprinkle with hazelnuts. Bake for 30 minutes or until firm.

Makes 8 servings.

Make Ahead: Refrigerate up to 3 days. Serve cold.

PEACH MERINGUE

This is a snap to prepare. To make individual servings, divide the peach mixture and meringue among 6 ovenproof ramekins.

4 cups	sliced peaches or 2 cans (14 oz each) sliced peaches (packed in juice), drained
1 tbsp + 1/2 cup	Splenda (optional)
1/2 tsp	cinnamon
3	egg whites
1/4 tsp	cream of tartar

1. Preheat oven to 300°F.
2. In large bowl, combine peaches, 1 tbsp Splenda, if using, and cinnamon. Spoon into pie plate or shallow baking dish.
3. In bowl, beat egg whites with cream of tartar until soft peaks form. Gradually beat in 1/2 cup Splenda until stiff peaks form.
4. Spread meringue over fruit, covering completely. Bake for 30 to 35 minutes or until golden. Serve immediately.

Makes 6 servings.

PANNA COTTA WITH BLUEBERRY SAUCE

Italian for "cooked cream," this silky eggless custard is a refreshing end to a meal. You can substitute blackberries for the blueberries if desired.

1 tbsp	powdered gelatin
3 tbsp	water
2 cups	skim milk
1/2 cup	Splenda
1 tsp	vanilla
1 cup	buttermilk
1/2 cup	non-fat yogurt, drained
	Blueberry Sauce (see below)

1. In small bowl, sprinkle gelatin over water and let soak for about 10 minutes (do not stir).
2. Meanwhile, in saucepan over medium heat, bring milk, Splenda and vanilla to simmer, stirring occasionally to dissolve Splenda. Remove from heat and add gelatin; stir until completely dissolved and mixture is smooth. Let cool to room temperature, about 30 minutes.
3. Stir buttermilk and yogurt into milk mixture. Strain through fine-mesh sieve and divide among 6 custard cups or ramekins. Refrigerate until panna cotta is set, at least 3 hours or up to 1 day. Run knife around sides of each panna cotta to loosen and invert onto serving plates, shaking gently to release onto plate. Spoon Blueberry Sauce around and over top of panna cotta.

Makes 6 servings.

Make Ahead: Refrigerate up to 1 day.

BLUEBERRY SAUCE

This sauce also makes a delicious topping for pancakes.

2 cups	fresh or frozen blueberries
1/4 cup	grape juice
3 tbsp	Splenda
2 tbsp	Grand Marnier or Triple Sec, optional

1. In saucepan, bring blueberries, grape juice, Splenda, and Grand Marnier, if using, to boil over medium-high heat. Continue to boil until Splenda is dissolved and berries are starting to burst. Transfer half of mixture to blender or food processor and purée until smooth. Return to mixture in saucepan and cook, stirring, for 2 minutes. Remove from heat and let cool to room temperature.

Makes about 2 cups.

Make Ahead: Refrigerate up to 2 days.

APPLE BURRITOS

These are very portable and may be enjoyed at room temperature. You can use pears in place of the apples. Serve with sweetened Yogurt Cheese (see recipe, page 248) or low-fat, no-sugar ice cream.

2 tsp	non-hydrogenated margarine
4 cups	sliced apples such as Cortland or Spy
3 tbsp	Splenda
1 tsp	cinnamon
1/2 tsp	ground ginger
1/2 cup	apple juice
1/2 cup	water
4	large whole wheat tortillas

1. Preheat oven to 350°F. Line a baking sheet with parchment paper.
2. In non-stick frying pan, melt margarine over medium-high heat. Add apples and sprinkle with Splenda, cinnamon and ginger. Pour in apple juice and water. Bring to boil and cook for 10 minutes or until apples are softened and juices are syrupy.
3. Place 4 tortillas on work surface. Divide apple filling among tortillas. Fold in sides and then roll up. Place seam side down on prepared baking sheet. Bake for 10 minutes or until golden brown.

Makes 4 servings.

Make Ahead: Wrap individually and freeze up to 1 month. Reheat from frozen in microwave or oven.

PLUM CRUMBLE

Crumbles are an ideal green-light dessert and can be made with a wide array of fruit. Try using pears instead of the plums and cut back slightly on the amount of Splenda.

1½ lb	prune plums (such as damson or Italian), halved and pitted
1 tbsp	Splenda
1 tbsp	cornstarch
½ tsp	ground ginger
½ tsp	cinnamon

Topping:

¾ cup	large-flake oats
½ cup	whole wheat flour
½ cup	Splenda
¼ cup	chopped almonds or pecans
¼ cup	non-hydrogenated margarine
1 tsp	grated orange zest
½ tsp	cinnamon
¼ tsp	ground cardamom

1. Preheat oven to 350°F.
2. In bowl, toss plums with Splenda, cornstarch, ginger and cinnamon. Arrange evenly in deep 9-inch pie plate.
3. Topping: In bowl, combine oats, flour, Splenda, almonds, margarine, orange zest, cinnamon and cardamom. Using your fingers, rub ingredients together until crumbly dough forms. Sprinkle evenly over fruit mixture. Bake for 35 to 40 minutes or until topping is golden and fruit mixture is bubbling.

Makes 6 servings.

Make Ahead: Refrigerate up to 2 days.

RHUBARB-GINGER COBBLER

Fresh rhubarb heralds the start of spring, but use frozen rhubarb to enjoy this homey heart-warming dessert year-round.

4 cups	chopped fresh or frozen rhubarb
1/2 cup	Splenda
2 tbsp	cornstarch
1 tbsp	grated fresh ginger

Topping:

1 cup	whole wheat flour
1 cup	large-flake oats
1/4 cup	Splenda
1 tbsp	baking powder
1 tsp	baking soda
1/4 tsp	salt
1/2 cup	liquid egg
1/2 cup	low-fat plain yogurt
1/2 cup	skim milk
1 tsp	vanilla

1. Preheat oven to 400°F. Oil an 8-inch square baking pan.
2. In bowl, toss together rhubarb, Splenda, cornstarch and ginger; spoon into prepared pan. Set aside.
3. Topping: In large bowl, combine flour, oats, Splenda, baking powder, baking soda and salt. In small bowl, whisk together egg, yogurt, milk and vanilla. Add to flour mixture and stir until just moistened. Drop topping by spoonfuls over fruit.
4. Bake for 25 to 30 minutes or until topping is golden and filling is bubbly. Let cool slightly before serving.

Makes 6 servings.

FRUIT AND CUSTARD PIE

This pie has a sinfully creamy texture.

1/2 cup	rolled oats
1/2 cup	almonds
3/4 cup	whole wheat flour
1/4 cup	unsweetened coconut
1/4 cup	ground flaxseed
2 tbsp	Splenda
1/2 tsp	salt
1/4 cup	canola oil
3 tbsp	cold water
1 tsp	vanilla

Filling:

2	omega-3 eggs
1 1/2 cups	low-fat plain yogurt
1/3 cup	Splenda
1 tsp	vanilla
1 1/2 cups	berries, cherries, chopped peaches or plums

1. Preheat oven to 350°F.
2. In food processor, chop oats and almonds until they resemble a coarse meal; transfer to bowl. Stir in flour, coconut, flaxseed, Splenda and salt.
3. In small bowl, whisk together oil, water and vanilla. Make well in centre of dry ingredients and pour in liquid; mix well to form dough. Press evenly into bottom and up sides of 9-inch tart pan with removable bottom. Bake for 15 minutes or until just firm and slightly golden. Let cool before filling.
4. **Filling:** In large bowl, whisk eggs, yogurt, Splenda and vanilla until smooth. Stir in fruit and pour into pie shell. Bake for 30 minutes or until filling is just set around edge and middle still jiggles. Chill for at least 2 hours before serving.

Makes 8 to 10 servings.

Make Ahead: Refrigerate up to 2 days.

RASPBERRY CREAM DACQUOISE

This is an impressive dessert to serve to guests.

1 cup	toasted blanched slivered almonds
2 tbsp	cornstarch
1 cup	Splenda
6	egg whites
1/4 tsp	cream of tartar
1 tsp	vanilla

Raspberry Cream Filling:

8 oz	light cream cheese, softened
2 cups	Yogurt Cheese (see recipe, page 248)
1/4 cup	Splenda
2 tbsp	orange juice
1 tbsp	orange zest
2 cups	raspberries (fresh or frozen)
	Fresh raspberries for garnish

1. Preheat oven to 275°F. Line 2 large baking sheets with parchment paper. Draw two 8-inch circles on each paper.
2. In food processor, chop almonds with cornstarch and 1/2 cup of the Splenda until finely ground.
3. In bowl, beat egg whites and cream of tartar until soft peaks form; gradually beat in remaining 1/2 cup Splenda until stiff, glossy peaks form. Beat in vanilla. Carefully fold in nut mixture. Spread evenly over circles.
4. Bake for 50 to 60 minutes or until firm to the touch. Using long metal spatula, carefully loosen meringues from parchment paper and transfer to wire rack; let cool completely.
5. **Raspberry Cream Filling:** In bowl, using electric mixer, beat together cream cheese, Yogurt Cheese, Splenda, orange juice and orange zest. Fold in raspberries.
6. Crumble least attractive meringue for garnish; set aside. Place 1 meringue in 9- or 10-inch springform pan. Spread with one-third of the filling. Repeat with remaining 2 meringues and filling. Sprinkle crumbled meringue over top. Cover with foil and freeze for at least 4 hours. Transfer to serving plate;

place in refrigerator for 45 minutes before serving to soften. Garnish with fresh raspberries.

Makes 10 to 12 servings.

Make Ahead: Store meringues in airtight container up to 1 week or wrap completed dacquoise well and freeze up to 3 days.

APPLE UPSIDE-DOWN CAKE

This cake is just as good made with pears. Serve warm with a scoop of low-fat, no-sugar ice cream or Sweetened Yogurt Cheese (see recipe, page 248).

3/4 cup	non-alcoholic apple cider or apple juice
6 cups	sliced peeled apples
1 cup	Splenda
1 tsp	cinnamon
1/2 tsp	ground ginger
1/4 tsp	ground cloves

Cake:

1/4 cup	non-hydrogenated margarine
3/4 cup	Splenda
1	omega-3 egg
1	egg white
1 tsp	vanilla
1 1/2 cups	whole wheat flour
1 tsp	baking powder
1 tsp	baking soda
1/2 tsp	ground ginger
1/4 tsp	salt
1/2 cup	buttermilk

1. Preheat oven to 350°F. Oil a 9-inch springform pan.
2. In large non-stick frying pan, heat apple cider over medium-high heat. Add apples, Splenda, cinnamon, ginger and cloves; toss to combine. Continue to cook, stirring occasionally, for 6 to 8 minutes or until liquid is absorbed and apples have softened slightly. Pour apples into bottom of prepared pan, spreading evenly. Set aside.
3. **Cake:** In bowl, beat margarine with Splenda until fluffy; beat in egg and egg white, 1 at a time. Beat in vanilla. In separate bowl, mix together flour, baking powder, baking soda, ginger and salt; stir half into margarine mixture. Stir in buttermilk, then remaining flour mixture. Pour into pan on top of apples, spreading evenly. Bake for 40 to 45 minutes or until top springs

back when lightly touched. Let cool in pan on rack for 15 minutes. Invert onto cake plate.

Makes 6 servings.

CARROT CAKE WITH CREAM CHEESE ICING

With the icing, this cake is scrumptious for birthdays or other celebrations. Without, it's still a special treat—a green-light one.

2 cups	whole wheat flour
2 tsp	baking powder
1 tsp	baking soda
2 tsp	cinnamon
1/2 tsp	ground ginger
1/2 tsp	salt
1/4 tsp	ground allspice
1/4 tsp	ground cardamom
1/4 tsp	ground nutmeg
1/2 cup	olive oil
3/4 cup	Splenda
1 tsp	vanilla
1/2 cup	liquid egg
2 cups	grated carrot
1	medium apple, cored and grated
1/2 cup	unsweetened applesauce
1/2 cup	juice-packed crushed pineapple, drained
1/2 cup	toasted chopped walnuts (optional)
	Cream Cheese Icing (see page 265)

1. Preheat oven to 350°F. Oil an 8- or 9-inch round cake pan; set aside.
2. In large bowl, mix together flour, baking powder, baking soda, cinnamon, ginger, salt, allspice, cardamom and nutmeg.
3. In separate bowl, beat together oil, Splenda and vanilla until smooth. Beat in egg. Stir in carrot, apple, applesauce, pineapple, and walnuts, if using. Pour over flour mixture and stir until moistened. Spread in prepared cake pan.
4. Bake for 45 to 50 minutes or until cake tester inserted in centre comes out clean. Let cool in pan on rack for 15 minutes. Run knife around edge of cake and invert onto rack to cool completely.

Makes 8 to 10 servings.

CREAM CHEESE ICING

4 oz	light cream cheese
1/4 cup	Yogurt Cheese (see recipe, page 248)
1 tbsp	Splenda (or to taste)
1 tbsp	frozen orange juice concentrate
1/2 tsp	vanilla

1. In bowl, beat together cream cheese, Yogurt Cheese, Splenda, orange juice concentrate and vanilla until smooth. Spread over top and sides of cake.

Makes about 2 cups.

Make Ahead: Refrigerate iced cake up to 2 days.

ONE-BOWL CHOCOLATE CAKE WITH GANACHE ICING

To make a layered birthday cake, cut this cake in half and spread 1/4 to 1/2 cup of the ganache between the layers before icing the top and sides. Without the ganache the cake is green light and still delicious.

	Canola oil
1 1/3 cups	whole wheat flour
3/4 cup	Splenda
1/2 cup	cocoa powder
1 1/2 tsp	baking soda
1 1/2 tsp	baking powder
1/2 tsp	salt
1	omega-3 egg
1	egg white
2/3 cup	buttermilk
1/2 cup	unsweetened applesauce
2 tbsp	canola oil
1 tsp	vanilla
	Grated zest of 1 orange

1. Preheat oven to 350°F. Oil an 8-inch round cake pan or springform pan. Cut out round of parchment paper and line bottom of pan.
2. In food processor or mixer, mix together all ingredients just until smooth.
3. Pour batter into pan, smoothing top. Bake for 20 to 25 minutes or until top springs back when lightly touched and cake tester inserted in centre comes out clean.
4. Allow to cool in pan on rack for 30 minutes. Remove from pan and remove parchment paper; let cool completely on rack.

Makes 6 to 8 servings.

GANACHE

8 oz	70% chocolate
$1\frac{1}{4}$ cups	low-fat soy milk

1. Melt chocolate in bowl set over barely simmering water. Remove from heat and whisk in soy milk until smooth.
2. Spread ½ cup ganache over top and sides of cake.

Makes 1½ cups.

Make Ahead: Refrigerate ganache up to 3 days or freeze up to 3 months. Melt in bowl set over barely simmering water before using.

ALMOND CHEESECAKE

Your guests won't guess that the secret ingredient in this cheesecake is tofu! Serve with fresh berries or with the berry filling from Berry-Stuffed French Toast (see recipe, page 216).

1/2 cup	toasted almonds, finely ground
1/2 cup	large-flake oats
1/2 cup	whole wheat flour
1/4 cup	Splenda
1/4 cup	non-hydrogenated margarine

Filling:

1 lb	firm tofu
3/4 cup	Splenda
1/2 cup	low-fat vanilla yogurt
2 tbsp	lemon juice
1	omega-3 egg
1 tbsp	almond extract
2 tsp	vanilla
1/4 tsp	salt

1. Preheat oven to 350°F.
2. In bowl, mix together almonds, oats, flour and Splenda. Using pastry cutter, 2 knives or your fingers, rub in margarine until mixture is crumbly. Pat into bottom of 8-inch springform pan. Bake for 15 minutes or until firm. Let cool. Reduce oven temperature to 325°F.
3. **Filling:** In food processor, purée all ingredients until smooth. Pour over crust.
4. Bake for 45 minutes or until filling is set. Remove from oven and run knife around edge to loosen. Allow to cool completely.

Makes 8 to 10 servings.

Make Ahead: Refrigerate up to 2 days.

STRAWBERRY OATMEAL SHORTCAKES

Celebrate the start of summer with fresh-picked strawberries and these old-fashioned biscuits.

1 cup	large-flake oats
1 cup	whole wheat flour
1/4 cup	wheat bran
1/4 cup	Splenda
1 tbsp	baking powder
1/2 tsp	baking soda
1/4 tsp	salt
1/3 cup	non-hydrogenated margarine
1/2 cup	non-fat sour cream
1/4 cup	skim milk
3 cups	sliced strawberries
2 cups	Sweetened Yogurt Cheese (see recipe, page 248)

Glaze:

1 tbsp	skim milk
1 tbsp	Splenda

1. Preheat oven to 400°F. Line a baking sheet with parchment paper.
2. In large bowl, combine oats, flour, bran, Splenda, baking powder, baking soda and salt. Cut in margarine until mixture is crumbly.
3. In another bowl, whisk together sour cream and milk. Add to flour mixture, stirring with fork to make a soft, sticky dough.
4. Turn out dough onto lightly floured surface and pat into circle about 1 inch thick. Using 3-inch cutter or overturned glass, cut dough into circles. Collect scraps and re-roll to cut 6 circles in total. Transfer rounds to prepared baking sheet.
5. **Glaze:** Brush shortcakes with milk and sprinkle with Splenda. Bake for 18 to 20 minutes or until golden brown. Transfer to rack to cool slightly.
6. To serve, slice shortcakes in half horizontally and spoon strawberries over bottom half. Top with a dollop of Sweetened Yogurt Cheese. Top with upper half and more strawberries and Sweetened Yogurt Cheese, if desired.

Makes 6 servings.

CRANBERRY-ALMOND BISCOTTI

Both pretty and delicious, these biscotti make festive treats. Wrap some in a clear plastic bag and tie with ribbon for a hostess gift. Whole wheat pastry flour gives the biscotti a more delicate texture, but if you can't find it, you can use regular whole wheat flour.

	Juice and zest of 1 orange
1 tbsp	Amaretto liqueur
1/2 cup	dried cranberries
1 1/2 cups	whole wheat pastry flour
1/2 cup	Splenda
1 tsp	cinnamon
1/2 tsp	baking powder
1/2 tsp	baking soda
1/4 tsp	ground nutmeg
1	omega-3 egg
1	egg white
1/2 cup	toasted almonds, chopped

1. Preheat oven to 350°F. Line a baking sheet with parchment paper.
2. In small saucepan, heat orange juice, Amaretto and cranberries just until hot. Remove from heat; let stand for 10 minutes. Drain, reserving juice.
3. In large bowl, mix together flour, Splenda, cinnamon, baking powder, baking soda and nutmeg.
4. In separate bowl, whisk together egg, egg white, orange zest and 2 tbsp reserved juice from cranberries; stir into dry mixture until combined, adding more juice if necessary to make dough moist. Stir in almonds and cranberries.
5. Transfer dough to prepared baking sheet. With lightly floured hands, press into 16-inch log; flatten slightly. Bake for 20 minutes or until firm. Let cool for 10 minutes on rack.
6. Reduce oven heat to 325°F. Cut log diagonally into 1/2-inch thick slices. Place on baking sheet, leaving 1 inch between biscotti. Bake until golden brown and crunchy, about 25 minutes. Let cool on rack.

Makes 20 cookies.

Make Ahead: Store in airtight container up to 1 week or wrap and freeze up to 3 months.

OATMEAL-CHOCOLATE CHUNK COOKIES

The oats make this dough a little crumbly when scooping. Don't worry—just squeeze it well with your fingers and it will stick together.

2 cups	large-flake oats
3/4 cups	whole wheat flour
1/4 cup	ground flaxseed
2 tsp	cinnamon
1 tsp	baking soda
1/2 tsp	baking powder
1/4 tsp	salt
1/2 cup	non-hydrogenated margarine
1/2 cup	Splenda
1	omega-3 egg
3 tbsp	water
2 tbsp	tahini
2 tsp	vanilla
2 oz	70% chocolate, chopped

1. Preheat oven to 350°F. Line a baking sheet with parchment paper.
2. In large bowl, stir together oats, flour, flaxseed, cinnamon, baking soda, baking powder and salt. Set aside.
3. In another bowl, beat margarine, Splenda, egg, water, tahini and vanilla until smooth. Stir oat mixture into margarine mixture until combined. Add chocolate and stir to combine.
4. Drop by heaping teaspoonfuls onto prepared baking sheet and flatten slightly. Bake for 10 to 12 minutes or until firm. Let cool on rack.

Makes about 24 cookies.

Make Ahead: Store in airtight container up to 3 days or freeze up to 1 month.

Variation: Substitute 1/2 cup dried currants, dried cranberries or chopped dried apricots for the chocolate.

CREAMY LEMON SQUARES

These tiny treats make an ideal mid-afternoon pick-me-up.

1/2 cup	whole wheat flour
1/2 cup	wheat bran
1/4 cup	ground almonds
1/4 cup	Splenda
1/4 cup	non-hydrogenated margarine

Filling:

1 cup	Splenda
3/4 cup	liquid egg
1/2 cup	lemon juice
1/4 cup	buttermilk
2 tsp	grated lemon zest
2 tsp	cornstarch
1 tsp	baking powder

1. Preheat oven to 350°F. Oil an 8-inch square baking pan.
2. In food processor or mixer, combine flour, bran, almonds and Splenda. Cut in margarine until mixture is crumbly.
3. Press mixture evenly into bottom of prepared baking pan. Bake for 20 to 25 minutes or until lightly browned. Set aside to cool.
4. **Filling:** In bowl, whisk together Splenda and egg. Stir in lemon juice, buttermilk, lemon zest, cornstarch and baking powder. Pour over base. Bake in 350°F oven for 15 to 20 minutes or until filling is set. Allow to cool to room temperature, then refrigerate for 2 hours before cutting into squares.

Makes 36 squares.

Make Ahead: Store in airtight container up to 3 days or freeze up to 1 month.

Seasonal Menus

Springtime Tea in the Garden

Lemony Lentil and Rice Soup, 57
Salmon, Red Potato and Asparagus Salad, 82
Tea-Infused Fruit Salad, 244
Strawberry Tea Bread, 239

Midsummer's Eve Barbecue

Mediterranean Summer Salad, 70
Black Bean Tabbouleh, 80
Spicy Roasted Chicken with Tomatoes and Tarragon, 164
Blueberry Beef Burgers, 174
Lemon Sour Cream Ice Cream with fresh berries, 247

Autumn Harvest Bistro Dinner

Mixed Greens with Roasted Pears, Pecans and Chèvre, 67
Blanquette de Veau, 182
Apple Upside-Down Cake, 262

Festive Season Buffet

Red Lentil Hummus with Basmati Rice Crackers, 31–32
Spinach Bites, 38
Fruit- and Nut-Stuffed Turkey Breast, 170
Vegetable Cassoulet, 110
Celeriac Slaw, 72
Cranberry-Almond Biscotti, 270

Index

Recipe Index

C

T